The
ROAD
of
HOPE

The
ROAD
of
HOPE

a gospel from prison

FRANCIS XAVIER
NGUYEN VAN THUAN

Translation and Introduction by John Peter Pham

WELLSPRING
North Palm Beach, Florida

wellspring

© 2013 F. X. Nguyen Van Thuan
Original title in Vietnamese Duong Hy Vong
© 1992 F. X. Nguyen Van Thuan
© 1997 Translation and Introduction John Peter Pham

This edition published 2018 by Wellspring.

Published with Permission of
New City Press 202 Comforter Blvd., Hyde Park, NY 12538
www.newcitypress.com

Design by Madeline Harris

ISBN: 978-1-929266-56-2 (hardcover)
ISBN: 978-1-63582-096-6 (ebook)

10 9 8 7 6 5 4 3 2 1

Printed in the United States of America

Seeing the crowds, he went up on the mountain, and when he sat down his disciples came to him. And he opened his mouth and taught them, saying:

"Blessed are the poor in spirit, for theirs is the kingdom of heaven.

"Blessed are those who mourn, for they shall be comforted.

"Blessed are the meek, for they shall inherit the earth.

"Blessed are those who hunger and thirst for righteousness, for they shall be satisfied.

"Blessed are the merciful, for they shall obtain mercy.

"Blessed are the pure in heart, for they shall see God.

"Blessed are the peacemakers, for they shall be called sons of God.

"Blessed are those who are persecuted for righteousness' sake, for theirs is the kingdom of heaven.

"Blessed are you when men revile you and persecute you and utter all kinds of evil against you falsely on my account. Rejoice and be glad, for your reward is great in heaven, for so men persecuted the prophets who were before you.

Matthew 5:1-12

CONTENTS

INTRODUCTION

Francois Xavier Nguyen Van Thuan:
A Profile in Witness, Truth, and Mission

The Concept of the Martyr

When one pauses to consider the immensity of human misery inflicted by human beings on other human beings in our century—the shocking crimes committed by individuals as well as nations, the mass extermination of peoples and the even crueler subjugation of others under the heel of totalitarianism—the difficulty of distinguishing Christian suffering from other forms of human misery, Christian victims from non-Christians becomes readily apparent. One might even ask whether there should be such a distinction.

This task is made all the more difficult by significant changes in the meaning of the once-specifically Christian designation of *martyr*. In the time of the early Fathers, the martyr was anyone who had testified to the truth of Christianity by steadfastness in faith despite hardships, peril, and even death. Later, although not always consistently, the designation became reserved for those who had sealed their faith with their blood during the persecutions. In either case, the use of the term *martyr* was limited to Christianity, and only to certain Christians at that.

There is no such reservation in modern usage. Gradually, any presumably innocent person killed on account of his religious, political, or moral convictions, whether a believer or not, became hailed as a martyr. Eventually, the person in question did not even have to die: he needed merely to demonstrate that he had experienced what is loosely defined as oppression. So the ranks of contemporary martyrs swell daily and range from the truly heroic (the Chinese student crushed by a tank in Tiananmen Square) to the downright banal (the self-styled artist who became a victim of censorship when he lost a government grant for some highly questionable works). Of these two changes, the second is acceptable insofar as it represents a return to an older tradition: the martyr is one who gives witness, even if he does not necessarily die in the process of proclaiming the truth. This is a particularly important development if humanity is to continue deriving inspiration from its martyrs—the increasingly delicate sensitivities of world opinion rarely permit outright murders any more, although systematic campaigns of oppression are occasionally ignored and allowed to run their course. The first change in concept, however, presents a problem for those seeking to differentiate Christian suffering from other human misery, the authentic Christian witness from other victims of modernity gone mad. Hans Urs von Balthasar attempted to resolve this difficulty in a little meditation written for the Eighty-fifth German Catholic Day in 1978, noting that:

If a Russian scholar, not wanting to submit to the degrading demands of the regime, puts up with the concentration camp or the insane asylum instead, then the proposition is evident to anyone: it is a matter of witnessing with one's life to the dignity and truth of the human being and of appealing to the conscience of humanity as a whole. But when a Christian dares to risk the same thing for his faith in Christ, the world knows, if it hears of the fact or pays attention to it, that the Christian suffers or dies for something that he regards as the all-sustaining truth of his life, something that, more profoundly than anything else, accounts for human dignity and human truth. Hence a martyrdom that is not only humanistic, but beyond that truly Christian, witnesses to the unabridged, integral New Testament faith. . . . With this condition fulfilled, one witness to the faith . . . who genuinely lives his mission can accomplish more than a hundred professional missionaries routinely pursuing their trade.[1]

We will never know the answer with certainty, but it would be interesting to speculate whether Father von Balthasar had ever heard of or paid any attention to—and hence, by his own logic, drawn some inspiration from—one such Christian witness, whose life and work is concisely summarized by the Swiss theologian those three key words: Witness, Truth, and Mission.

---

[1] Hans Urs von Balthasar, *New Elucidations* (San Francisco: Ignatius, 1986), pp. 293, 300–01.

Witness

That witness, Francois-Xavier Nguyen Van Thuan, was born on April 17, 1928, in Hue, then the imperial capital of Vietnam. Young Francois-Xavier was a scion of one of Vietnam's oldest Catholic families. His branch of the great Nguyen clan, which could boast over three hundred years of the faith, had nearly been destroyed during the nineteenth-century persecutions of the fourth Nguyen emperor, Tu Due. At the time of his birth, however, the fires of persecution had long abated, although memories of the dark hours were still kept alive by relatives who had survived the ordeal.

Francois-Xavier's family fared well in those years and he was born into a privileged position in one of Vietnam's most prominent families, which numbered among its members Ngo dinh Diem, first President of the Republic of Vietnam, and Pierre-Martin Ngo dinh Thuc, Archbishop of Hue, the boy's uncles.

Despite the grand opportunities open to a young man from such a background, Francois-Xavier discovered a vocation to the priesthood, fired particularly by his youthful involvement in the Eucharistic Crusade, a popular Vietnamese Catholic movement promoting Eucharistic devotion and apostolic work during those years. He entered the Major Seminary at Hue and was ordained a priest on June 11, 1953. After several years of pastoral work, he was sent to Rome in 1956 to study canon law at the Athenaeum of the Propaganda Fide (now the Pontifical University Urbaniana), receiving his doctorate in 1959.

Returning to Vietnam, he served as professor and then rector of the Seminary of the Archdiocese of Hue. He was nominated

Bishop of Nha Trang, a maritime city 270 miles north of Saigon, on April 24, 1967, by Pope Paul VI and consecrated on June 24 of that year, the feast of the Birth of St. John the Baptist. As he was later to observe, "Almost all the key dates in my life have coincided with the Church's major feasts."

At Nha Trang, true to his motto of *Gaudium et spes*, he served happily for eight years despite the war which was raging around him. As he later noted, he was deeply conscious of the Second Vatican Council's mandate to "give witness to Christ in the ordinary circumstances of everyday life, and to bring the Church into the world." To this end, he was particularly active in encouraging theological formation programs for the laity and educational and other social works. Among the many fruits of his labor, the over seven hundred priestly vocations he fostered in eight years stands as an unparalleled testimony to his pastorate in a post-Conciliar period plagued with a general crisis in the number of vocations.

While maintaining a busy pastoral schedule in his own diocese, he found time during those years also to serve the Church in Vietnam at large, serving as chairman of the Vietnamese Episcopal Conference commissions for social communications and development. In the latter capacity, he also became a well-known figure outside Vietnam with frequent trips abroad to solicit aid for the reconstruction efforts in his war-plagued country. He was one of the founders of Radio Veritas, the Catholic broadcast network which serves all of Asia.

From 1968 to 1974, he served as a member of the Pontifical Council of the Laity. At the request of Pope Paul VI, he also traveled widely during those years promoting efforts toward a peaceful resolution of the Vietnamese conflict. The war had taken its toll on the Bishop and his flock, with the priests and faithful alike killed by bombardments from both sides and numerous churches destroyed. But as he notes, "We wanted peace, yet it had to be a just peace which would not be disadvantageous to the church."

On April 23, 1974, a week before the communist victory in the conflict was complete, he was named Titular Archbishop of Vadesi and Coadjutor Archbishop of Saigon, the capital of the faltering Vietnamese Republic. The aged Archbishop, Paul Nguyen Van Binh, who had weathered the war years, was without episcopal assistance at the time and had petitioned Rome for the nomination of a coadjutor to assist him with the tasks that lay ahead with the reconstruction. The communists, however, interpreted the appointment differently, denouncing it as a "conspiracy between the Vatican and the imperialists" to place the popular Bishop Nguyen Van Thuan in Saigon to be the head of an anti-communist resistance movement.

The new Coadjutor Archbishop left for his new see of Saigon on May 8, 1975, after having consecrated and installed his successor in Nha Trang. He was immediately intercepted by communist officials who ordered him to return to Nha Trang and to content himself with being bishop there. When he replied that, having installed a new bishop there, he no longer enjoyed any canonical rights there and thus could not turn back, he was taken into custody. On August 15, the feast of the Assumption, he was deported to a small village where he was incarcerated in the parish church while the authorities planned their next move.

Meanwhile the communist government had begun its systematic campaign against the Church in Vietnam. Priests, especially former military chaplains and human rights advocates, and religious were being rounded up and deported to a new system of "re-education camps." Churches and other ecclesiastical property were either summarily confiscated or otherwise rendered unfit for use. The majority of bishops were put under house arrest, if not imprisoned outright. Although for the most part Vietnamese Catholics responded to this persecution with the same patient and faithful endurance with which their ancestors met the imperial edicts of the previous century, there was one attempt at armed resistance in the parish of St. Vincent in Saigon. Disregarding the fact that the Archbishop had been incarcerated some 300 miles away for the past six months, the government seized upon the failed effort as "evidence" of his "conspiracy" and formally arrested him on March 18, 1976, the vigil of the feast of St. Joseph.

The Archbishop was deported to North Vietnam on November 1, 1976, the Feast of All Saints, along with two thousand other prisoners destined for "re-education camps."

The next thirteen years of his life were spent in the various prisons and "re-education camps" of the communist government, including long periods (amounting, in total, to nine years) in isolation cells. The Archbishop prefers not to say much about this period, as if afraid that the result would be personal glorification and detract from the Truth to whom he bears witness. When pressed to speak about his experience, he can only say:

The hardest thing, above all else, was that I began [to] feel helpless—my plans, my efforts, and my activities were all for nothing. This "practical helplessness" describes my condition for thirteen years. I wanted to do so many things, to serve my people, but I could not. Then I came to think about Jesus on the Cross: that he was immobilized, he could neither preach nor administer any sacraments—he, too, was "helpless." Nevertheless, it was from there that he performed his greatest deed: he redeemed us sinners. Thanks to his help, I have never regretted my destiny.

Finally, under pressure from numerous international groups, Archbishop Van Thuan was formally released from prison on November 21, 1988, the Feast of the Presentation of the Virgin Mary. Nevertheless, he was still prohibited from entering the Archdiocese of Saigon and was placed under de facto house arrest in the capital, Hanoi, where he was forbidden to celebrate any sacraments publicly. There he remained until December 1991, when the government unexpectedly expelled him from Vietnam. The Archbishop resided in Rome from November 24, 1994, the Feast of the Martyrs of Vietnam, until his death on September 16, 2002. During that time he served on the Pontifical Council for Justice and Peace, acting as its president from 1998–2002.

Truth

The years of imprisonment were difficult ones, not only for the Archbishop, but also for the Church in Vietnam. It was against this background that *The Road of Hope* was born. In 1975 while the government was preparing its case against him, the Archbishop was kept under house arrest in the isolated village of Cay

Vong. Realizing that this "respite" would be brief and that the Church, bereft of its shepherds, was facing a period of possibly years of persecution, the Archbishop took up his pen. Originally, he intended to write short messages of encouragement to his orphaned flock and to include in them a few practical spiritual counsels. However, as he continued writing, the scope of the work grew until, toward the end of 1975, he had a full-fledged manuscript.

The full story of the manuscript will not be told while the communist government continues to hold sway in Vietnam. However, with much effort and sacrifice on the part of dedicated lay leaders formed by the Archbishop during his years as Bishop of Nha Trang, the pages were smuggled out of his imprisonment and clandestinely reassembled and printed as *Duong Hy Vong* (The Road of Hope). The little book of some 1,001 short pensées, intended to be read within the context of Scripture and the Church's teachings, proved to be instantly popular with the Vietnamese people, many of whom, like the author, were suffering a living martyrdom for their faith.

Despite government efforts to halt the work, it only spread. Vietnamese, Christians and non-Christians alike, carried it with them everywhere, even into the prisons, bringing with them its messages of hope. Eventually copies accompanied the great flight abroad which became known as the "Boat People" phenomenon. While its author was still imprisoned, translations were made from these clandestinely printed copies into French and English, and likewise met with instant popularity. The present edition was initiated in Rome at the initiative of the Archbishop who wanted to revise and edit the book, an opportunity which was denied him during his imprisonment. Thus the text represents the definitive form of *The Road of Hope* as envisioned by the author.

Mission

The author of *The Road of Hope* reveals himself in its pages as a firm exponent of the doctrine that all baptized Christians are called to be sent as apostles to the nations, each in his own time and place. In so doing, the Archbishop offers an insight into his episcopal motto, "*Gaudium et spes*": he calls upon all to fulfill their baptismal commitment and to advance through life as along a road of hope, followed in joy. The spiritual itinerary of this road is simultaneously evangelical, ecclesial, and humane. As such it is faithful to the Second Vatican Council's exhortation to all Christians:

> Mindful of the words of the Lord: "By all this men will
> know that you are my disciples, if you have love for one
> another," (John 13:35) Christians can yearn for nothing
> more ardently than to serve the men of this age with an
> ever-growing generosity and success. Holding loyally to the
> Gospel, enriched by its resources, and joining forces with
> all who love and practice justice, they have shouldered a
> weighty task here on earth and they must render an account
> of it to him who will judge all men on the last day. . . . It is
> the Father's will that we should recognize Christ our brother
> in the persons of all men and love them with an effective

---

[2] *Gaudium et spes*, 93.

love, in word and deed, thus bearing witness to the truth. . . .
In this way men all over the world will awaken to a lively
hope (the gift of the Holy Spirit) that they will one day be
admitted to the haven of surpassing peace and happiness in
their homeland radiant with the glory of the Lord.[2]

For Christians, the Council has thus concisely explained the
inner logic of their unique vocation: to announce to all by their
very lives that Christ is indeed "the way, and the truth, and the
life" (John 14:6).

It should be noted, in concluding, that *The Road of Hope*
was intended as neither a theological treatise nor a spiritual
manual in the strict sense of the term. What it was to be, however, was a message of encouragement from an imprisoned father to his children. It was an appeal from a pastor to his flock to
persevere in his absence, to continue witnessing to the truth by
letting their lives express the faith their lips professed. The style
of the work may seem at times to be "foreign": the author speaks
directly to his readers with a certain familiarity touched with an
occasional wry humor. But then, could it be otherwise between
a father and his children?

In following the Road of Hope sketched here, may readers
come to know the hope and experience the joy which Christ
intended for all of his disciples to share.

—John Peter Pham

TRANSLATOR'S PREFACE TO THE ENGLISH EDITION

This present volume, the definitive English translation of *The Road of Hope*, has benefited greatly from the encouragement, help, and, most importantly, prayers which I received from a number of individuals.

First and foremost, I would like to thank His Excellency Archbishop Francois-Xavier Nguyen Van Thuan for honoring me with the task of editing and translating this edition of his book. It is my hope that, in presenting this edition of *The Road of Hope* to its author, I may in some small way render tribute to his heroic service to Christ and his Church.

Although I am indebted to all who, in whatever way, aided me in this endeavor, several people deserve special mention.

I am also pleased to acknowledge the translators of the previous editions of *The Road of Hope* whose works—although in many instances substantially different from this one in both content and scope—consulted in the preparation of this edition: Mr. Paul Bookalil (English) and Fr. Jean Mais (French). The

Reverend Paul Phan Van Hien, a long-time collaborator with the Archbishop, also provided important assistance.

During this project, as well as in a host of other endeavors, I was greatly helped by the fatherly good will and support of my ordinary, the Most Reverend John J. Myers, Bishop of Peoria.

I am deeply grateful to the faculty and staff and to my fellow students of the Pontifical French Seminary and the Pontifical North American College—Casa Santa Maria for their patient forbearance with and many kindnesses to me during the period I was engaged with this work.

Finally, I would be remiss if I failed to acknowledge the courageous Church in Vietnam which originally inspired the author to write this book and many of whose sons and daughters, like him, have suffered long imprisonment as confessors for the faith. May the dark night of persecution soon be dispelled by the light of a new day of hope.

For all those, named and unnamed, who assisted me in this work in any way, and for those who seek counsel in its pages, I invoke the loving intercession of the Mother of God and our mother: O Mary, conceived without sin, pray for us who have recourse to thee!

—John Peter Pham

PROLOGUE

The Road of Hope

My child,

I have traveled along life's road,
where I have experienced both joys and sorrows;
but always I have been overflowing with hope
because I have our Lord and his mother Mary by
my side.

If the Lord permits me to choose again,
I would not choose any other road but this.
I have been happy and full of joy because I have
hope in the Lord and I have learned to love.

Today, as our Lord gives me a few moments to be
close to his side,
I shall begin to record for you,
as I have wanted to do for a long time, the experiences of my life.
I approach this task with a feeling of humility.

These are the words of a father, a father who does
not have anything new to say to his child.

This father simply repeats some words of advice
which come truly from the heart, words which so
many times before have been gently poured
into your ear and heart
in the midst of the noisy activity of the world
around you.

It is my earnest hope
that these simple thoughts may spread light and
peace so that you may become an apostle animated
with a spirit of prayer and a spirit of love.

May the grace and peace of our Lord be with you
on this journey of hope!

Your father,
+ Francois Xavier

One: Departure

If you are still bound by a gold chain,
you are not ready for this road.

1. Our Lord guides you on to this road so that you will "go and bear fruit" (John 15:16) which will endure. The road is called *The Road of Hope* because it is overflowing with hope and is as beautiful as hope itself. And why should you not have hope when it is the Lord Jesus himself with whom you set off on the way to the Father?

2. The itinerary for this Road of Hope has three stages:

- Departure: Renounce yourself.
- Duty: Take up your cross daily.
- Perseverance: Follow me.

3. If you have given up everything, but still have not denied yourself, you have actually not given up anything at all. Unless you give up yourself, you will—slowly perhaps, but surely—gather to yourself once again those very things which you gave up in the first place.

4. Abraham set off on his journey with the hope of reaching the promised land. Moses set off with the hope of rescuing the People of God from their slavery. Our Lord Jesus Christ came down from heaven with the hope of saving all mankind.

5. What difference does it make if you leave home for some distant place, perhaps even thousands of miles away, if you continue to bring along all your bad habits, your sinful self?

6. Saints are "fools for Christ's sake" (1 Corinthians 4:10). Thus, the making of saints is beyond the scope of the wisdom of the world.

7. If you wish to set off on this road, you must go regardless of what other people may say to ridicule you. The Three Magi set off hoping to find the newborn Savior, and they found him. St. Francis Xavier set off hoping to save souls, and he found them. St. Maria Goretti set off to resist temptation, hoping thus to meet her Lord, and she met him.

8. You must lose in order to gain, die in order to live, abandon all else in order to meet the Lord. The Magi risked dangers and ridicule; St. Francis Xavier left his parents and country,

forsaking worldly possessions and pleasure forever; St. Maria Goretti gave up her life.

9. Keep going forward on the Road of Hope, regardless of the often heartrending pleas of those you love. St. Paul knew that "imprisonment and afflictions await me" (Acts 20:23) and Jesus himself foresaw that the road to Jerusalem would lead to his great Passion (see Matthew 16:21). Yet both continued onwards.

10. Rich or poor, praised or ridiculed, noble or lowly—your station in life does not matter at all if you have decided to advance along this road, waiting in joyful hope for the coming of our Savior Jesus Christ.

11. Our Lord declared, "I am the truth" (John 14:6). He did not say that newspapers are the truth, radio is the truth, or television is the truth. Which truth will you follow?

12. Keep moving forward relentlessly. Do not give up. Nobody will follow the person who turns back.

13. Do not give in to sensuality, do not give in to laziness, do not give in to selfishness. You cannot call black white, bad good, or dishonesty truth.

14. Are you a person who says "yes" to everything? Do you perhaps say "yes" to many gods, many religions, and a variety of

moral "standards"? Do you have a flexible conscience which can accommodate itself to any situation and say "yes" to its values? Which road will you take?

15. Refusal to give in to false values is neither pride nor egoism nor stubbornness. Rather, it proves your wholehearted adherence to your own standards.

16. You should be prepared to reject wealth and position—to give your very life if necessary—to preserve your ideals, your honor, and, most importantly, your faith. Never behave otherwise: To do so would be to lose everything.

Two: Duty

Duty is the passport to heaven.

17. Duty points out the will of God for you in the present moment.

18. Some people do not shoulder the cross because they imagine it to be too heavy. Still other people are eager to shoulder everyone else's cross but refuse to carry their own and even seek to foist it on to another person's shoulders.

19. Make your duties holy. Help others to holiness through your duties. Grow in holiness by the way you carry out your duties.

20. If everyone were faithful to their duties in life, growth in personal holiness would, while renewing their own hearts, also renew their families and the whole world around them.

21. Despite any superficial appearance of holiness, a person who neglects his duties in life is a spiritual fraud. Should he work "miracles," they will be both out of time and out of place and a cause of confusion, not edification. Moreover, such a person would be difficult to live with.

22. Some laypeople associate holiness with formal prayer, preaching, or withdrawal from the world: They mistakenly draw this image from a past period in the Church's history.

On the other hand, some priests and religious today conceive of holiness in terms of social or political action; they end up competing with laypeople. How chaotic!

23. The world is not being renewed because people continue to conceive of holiness as something other than carrying out the duties of their state in life.

24. The workman will become a saint in the workplace, the soldier will become a saint in the army, the patient will become a saint in the hospital, the student will become a saint through his studies, the farmer will become a saint on the farm, the politician will become a saint in government office, and the priest will become a saint by faithfully fulfilling his priestly ministry. Every step of progress along the road to sanctity is a step of sacrifice in the performance of one's duty.

25. Saints do not become saints through acts of prophecy or performance of miracles. They do nothing extraordinary at all, other than faithfully carrying out their ordinary duties.

26. The duty of the present moment, however, is not to be regarded as something passive. Rather, it is a constant and unceasing self-renewal, decision to choose or reject the Lord, search for the kingdom of God, belief in the infinite love of God, ardent action from the heart, reflection of the love of God in love of others—all in the present moment.

27. Duty is your passport to heaven.

28. Accept the will of God, obey the will of God, or love the will of God. Which way will you choose?

29. If our Lord wants you to endure some disgrace because of your duty, he will at the same time give you part of the honor of his holy cross.

30. Let your response be: "O Lord, the place of my duty is Calvary and I am the offering."

31. In order to become a saint, you need only to fulfill your duty in the present moment. The revelation and discovery of this simple fact should give your soul peace and encouragement.

32. Your last duty will be death, which you must accept willingly and lovingly.

33. As you advance in appreciating the sanctifying value of your ordinary duties, you will come to appreciate that the yoke is indeed easy and the burden light (cf. Matthew 11:30).

34. There are three possible reasons why your soul is worried and disconcerted:

- You have set low standards for the performance of your duties.
- You are not following the will of God.
- You limit the extent to which you are willing to follow the will of God.

35. If you are not firmly attached to the will of God, you will begin to think that your duty is too uneventful, too unnoticed and hidden. When you begin to regard the performance of your ordinary duties as monotonous, then you will also begin to fall by the wayside of this Road of Hope.

36. The problem and its solution is a very simple one. Before doing anything, ask our Lord, "What is it that I must do?" (see Acts 22:10). The answer will always be: "Carry out the will of God."

37. If God desires it to rain, desire the same. If God desires the sun to shine, desire the same. If God desires to make things pleasant, desire the same. If God desires to visit you with hardship and travail, desire the same.

And rejoice, for to have but one will with God is the secret of happiness.

38. In our everyday lives, our Lord constantly offers us the happiness of participating in the mystery of redemption. But the road to Calvary lies on the road of duty.

Three: Perseverance

*Anyone can begin, but only the saints
persevere to the end.*

39. If you desire to reach the end of this Road of Hope, you will have to be fearless and courageous. How many people followed our Lord Jesus Christ to the end of his road and could be found beside him at the foot of the cross?

40. Do not be afraid to confide all your desires to Jesus. Remember his promise: "Hitherto you have asked nothing in my name. Ask and you will receive, that your joy may be full" (John 16:24). To be truly fearless is to love as a child loves its father.

41. Do not allow failures to discourage you. If you are seeking to do God's will and meet with some setback, that "failure" is a success in the eyes of God, for it occurred in the act of doing his will. Look at the example of Jesus on the cross.

42. Results and success are two entirely different things. There may be no outward sign of results, but at the same time there can be an increase in experience, humility, and faith in God—and these are the signs of success from a supernatural point of view.

43. There is only one failure and that is to fail to hope in God. Hope in God and you will not be disappointed (see Psalm 30).

44. Do not be a "fair weather saint"; the inevitable storms of life will wipe out the externals and reveal the sinfulness behind the appearance.

45. The virtuous person radiates sweetness quietly and unobtrusively.

46. Be actively loyal as you travel along this road. Peter did not betray our Lord, nor did he accuse him. On the other hand, he was passive: not lifting a finger to acknowledge or support Jesus—not even uttering one word. Rather, seeking to remain safe and to avoid being implicated, he declared that he did not even "know the man" (see Matthew 26:72). Peter had lost hope in our Lord as the Way and fled from him.

47. You tremble with fear. You have stumbled and fallen. You have met with difficulties, misunderstandings, criticism, disgrace, perhaps even a sentence of death. You despair, but why do you forget the gospel? Our Lord Jesus Christ suffered everything. But if you continue to follow him, you too will have your Easter triumph.

48. Every morning when you rise, you begin life anew—fresh, energetic, and full of optimism. If the day runs badly, continue to persevere along the road with our Lord as did the two downcast disciples on the road to Emmaus. Like them, you will reach your goal.

49. Perseverance is the characteristic of saints, because "he who endures to the end will be saved" (Matthew 10:22).

50. Even if everyone else should fall by the wayside on this journey, you must continue pressing forward. The masses are easily seduced; a leader who guides wisely is rare. You must have the strength of character to refuse to follow the crowd blindly.

51. Although you may feel worn out or less enthused, keep your spirits up. The dark clouds cannot block the sunlight forever; they will pass. Just wait for them to pass over.

52. Do not say, "I no longer feel inspired." Why should you work because of human inspiration? The work of God is in no way comparable with the writing of poetry. Work because of love and the knowledge of the fact that you will never lose the love of God.

53. The good thief achieved happiness because of his hope in the love of God; Judas was wretched because he despaired of this same love (see Matthew 27:5; Luke 23:42–3).

54. In his darkest hour, Jesus cried out, "My God, my God, why hast thou forsaken me?" (Matthew 27:46) At that moment, his

mother stood by his cross. She was silent, but her steadfast love was great enough to support her son until he said, "It is finished" (John 19:30).

55. The body of the widow of Nain's son was being carried out for burial (see Luke 7:12) and that of Lazarus was already decaying in the grave (see John 11:39), but the Lord could still call on both to rise from the dead. Have hope and humbly repent of your sins; Jesus will also raise you up.

56. Every day, decrease your self-centeredness and increase your love of your neighbor. Every day, lessen your reliance on yourself and increase your trust in God.

57. If you are determined not to persevere, it is not because you are meek, but because you are a coward.

58. You keep complaining, "If only I were in this or that place, if only I could work with this or that person and hold this or that office, surely I would succeed." No! Do the work the Lord has entrusted to you. You are exactly where he wants you; proceed from there. If you continue to bustle about in every other direction, you will never reach the end.

59. In your soul are two persons, John and Judas. Whenever you are striving to persevere, you are following the loyal, faithful John. Whenever you cravenly give up the struggle, you are choosing Judas as your patron and you are burning incense, as it were, in honor of that patron of traitors.

60. You say that it is too difficult. This may be true enough, but only something acquired through great effort will be truly worthwhile.

Four: The Call: Vocation

Mobilize all your strength to follow God's call.

61. "Follow me . . ." (Matthew 9:9). The apostles gave up everything to follow the Lord. Like them, will you decide once and for all to follow his call, or will he have to keep calling over and over again?

62. Making a decision will always involve some uncertainty, some risk. Pause and ponder the matter if you need to, but you must eventually come to a decision.

63. Jesus is clear about the total, radical dedication he requires: "If any man would come after me, let him deny himself and take up his cross daily and follow me" (Luke 9:23). Elsewhere he says, "If anyone comes to me and does not hate his own father and mother and wife and children and brothers and sisters, yes, even his own life, he cannot be my disciple" (Luke 14:26).

The road has been clearly defined. The call is clear and unambiguous.

64. "Go and preach the gospel" (Mark 16:15). The Lord requires that those who dare to accept this lofty mission have a readiness to die, that is, courage in the face of death. Looking back on the two thousand years of the Church's history, we can see that there has never been a lack of people, in every time and from every class, willing to die for the gospel.

65. There are some people who throughout their lives rely on other people to make decisions for them. Are you one of these?

66. Perhaps you want to retreat because you have either suffered personal setbacks or become disheartened on seeing that some other people have not been able to endure similar difficulties and trials. But whom will you follow: the Lord or these other people?

67. Why are you so surprised that so many willingly follow the call of the Lord, even if it means suffering and death? Remember his promise: "Lo, I am with you always, to the close of the age" (Matthew 28:20).

68. Other people will never understand why we follow the Lord's call and will think that we are mad. Even Jesus was called mad. We should therefore be proud to be able to share in such a divine insanity.

69. Your decision to follow our Lord does not happen when you sign your documents or pronounce your vows. Rather, it consists of the endless day-to-day struggle involved in following his call throughout the entire course of your life.

70. "Lo, we have left everything and followed you. What then shall we have?" (Matthew 19:27). You have given up everything to follow our Lord who in turn has now become your special protector. Why are you worrying about anything?

71. Do not be surprised if, while you are following Jesus, you should hear calls from all manner of sources (pleasure, reputation, your body, parents, among other things) to abandon the road you are on. Still, keep on going and remember the Lord's warning: "No one who puts his hand to the plough and looks back is fit for the kingdom of God" (Luke 9:62).

72. "Follow me . . ." (Matthew 9:9). This call will continue to remind you of your commitment during every little task you perform and your constant "yes" to it must endure until your last breath.

73. It may seem easy to say "yes," but remember that Jesus showed us that a "yes" entails a road to Calvary, to the cross. Deny yourself, carry your cross daily, nail yourself to that cross.

74. Our Lord commands you to "go into all the world and preach the gospel to the whole creation" (Mark 16:15). But he

did not issue a timetable or draw up any logistical details. He leaves it to you to take the initiative in this journey of life, asking only that you remember always to carry the gospel along with you in your endeavors.

75. The Second Vatican Council teaches us the importance of being truly "radical" by going back to the sources, rediscovering the lives of the apostles, those who lived with Jesus, listened to him, had personal contact with him, and then witnessed to him.

76. A program that is going well has to be left unfinished, some zealous activities are reduced to inactivity, some important mission has to be scaled down in scope—you become upset and discouraged. But remember: Did Jesus ask you to follow him or to follow this work or that person? Leave these things to the Lord and he will work everything out for the best.

77. You do not trust anyone else, you do not delegate responsibility to anyone else, you do not yield your position to anyone else. Do you consider yourself even more powerful than God himself who has deigned to give us a share in his work?

78. Why are you so attached to this or that task that you refuse to relinquish it, even when your superiors wish to transfer you to other duties? The work belongs to the Lord more than it belongs to you: It is his concern.

79. The most dangerous moment in apostolic work is when the apostle begins to experience self-satisfaction. This is the time when the devil concentrates all his forces to take us by surprise.

Five: The Interior Life

The contemplative life is realized in your actions.

80. Peace depends on victory, and victory depends upon struggle. If you desire peace, you will have to fight continually.

81. In this struggle, your weapons are meditation, self-denial, the sacraments, the rosary, and recollection. Your allies are Mary, St. Joseph, the angels, your patron saints, and your spiritual director. Unless you gradually drop your weapons or abandon your allies, your victory is assured.

82. If you stand on an upper story of a tall building and look down on the city below, you will see streams of people running around in all directions. You will see a mass of vehicles and people fighting each other, frantically hurrying around in circles—all for the sake of money, ambition, or competition.

Only when we fearlessly throw ourselves (with at least as much force as these poor people) into the work of God will we have a faith that is truly alive and a fervent apostolic spirit.

83. If you were to resolve to improve on the practice of just one virtue each year, and if you would work on that particular virtue every day, very soon you would achieve great improvement.

84. A diver will plunge deep into the dark ocean and an astronaut will launch far into uncharted space for the cause of science. Can you do any less for our Lord? When you have given up everything for Jesus, even to the point of risking your life, then the authenticity of your interior life will be evident to others.

85. You wish to set the whole world on fire with the love which the gospel teaches; you wish to conquer the five continents. Then your every moment should be a flash of fire, the fire of duty, obedience, and patience. Such a flame will burn bright and illumine the whole world.

86. External silence and, even more importantly, interior silence are necessities for the interior life.

87. You do not have to be learned or extraordinarily talented to become holy. All you need is the grace of God and your own determination. Yet the reason so few people become saints is because it is easier to become learned than to change one's whole life in order to become holy.

88. Although you may be eager to serve God well, unless this enthusiasm is accompanied by a deep personal renewal, your sacrifice will not be pleasing to him.

89. Worldly people are frightened by silence because they feel empty when alone. On the other hand, those who live an interior life value silence because in it they discover a new and more beautiful world: a life of intimacy with the Trinity, a life which this world cannot give.

90. Do not confuse the work of God with God himself. There will be times when the Lord will want you to choose him first and to leave the work in his hands.

91. You want to know when you have to start living this interior life? You must start this very moment and start anew each and every day of your life.

92. Who must be holy? Everybody without exception is called to holiness. But start with yourself.

93. In this world, there is nothing as precious as divine grace. With it, heaven has already begun in your heart even as you are still in the world.

94. Each precious, sparkling diamond is formed in a mass of rock in the depths of the earth over millions of years. Do you mature from within in the same way?

95. Spread throughout the world and proclaim loudly: "There is one man who has laid down his life for his friends."

96. The raging fire on the movie screen frightens some people, but it neither burns hot nor can it cook anything. It is only the image of a fire and does not issue from a red-hot furnace.

97. Our love of God must be absolute. Our Lord teaches us that no one can serve two masters at the same time (see Matthew 6:24). How many masters do you serve?

98. Set aside a few moments every day to focus especially on advancing in your interior life.

99. Some people look at the Church today and see a crisis of faith. Others see a crisis of authority. Actually there is only one crisis: It is a crisis of holiness. God sends us these trials in order to refine us, separating the good from the bad.

100. You might find it difficult to understand St. Augustine's prayer: "Lord, let me know you, let me know myself." However, his reason can be found in Jesus' question: "Have I been with you so long, and yet you do not know me, Philip?" (John 14:9). If we arrive at the point where we truly know him, our lives will have changed completely.

101. There are people whose practice of the faith consists only in reciting many prayers and attending many Masses, but these have yet to put their faith into practice. This is no different from

someone who might ask a friend if he is well, only to receive in reply, "I eat six meals a day." Eating meals is not necessarily the same thing as good health. In fact, it is often the opposite.

Six: The Supernatural Life

*The supernatural life consists in a wholehearted
commitment to the will of God.*

102. If everyone, except God, should approve of your conduct,
you are to be pitied! If, on the other hand, you should be insulted,
falsely accused, and persecuted by everyone else, but are praised
by God, happy are you for the kingdom of heaven is yours!

103. What use is it if everyone affirms you, but God disapproves
of you? If everybody should mock you, but God affirms you,
happy are you! When the crowd cried out, "Release to us Barabbas!" (Luke 23:18), Barabbas remained a robber all the same.
When that same crowd shouted "Crucify him!" (Luke 23:21),
our Lord was still the sinless Son of God.

104. If you are faced with ungrateful people who have betrayed
you or falsely accused you, what hurts you the most is the

irrational malice which has poured out of those from whom you have least expected it. Nevertheless, your reaction should be:

- To forgive right from the heart.
- To beg forgiveness for your enemies.
- To pray with love that they be converted.

In this way, you will not need to rely on the consolation of the world.

105. Rejoice at your success, but thank God that someone else has been more successful than you.

106. What is foolish in the eyes of men is wisdom in the eyes of God.

107. The cross of Christ may have appeared foolish to the Jews and been a stumbling block to the Greeks, but it is our glory.

108. Spending your whole day in church does not necessarily make you holy if, when you leave, you continue to criticize others, to react according to the wisdom of the world, or to remain self-centered. Remember, James and John were with Jesus often, yet he still had to reprimand them for their attitude toward the inhospitable Samaritan town (see Luke 9:51–55).

109. Do not simply say, "I follow my conscience." First, what kind of conscience is it that you follow?

110. Poverty, obedience, mortification, meekness, charity, forgiveness, humility—all these virtues are considered foolish in the eyes of the world. They are, however supremely important in the eyes of God. What the world regards as a misfortune, God considers true happiness.

111. If you learned to look at everything from God's point of view, you would see different values and new dimensions.

112. In all the maneuvers and struggles you may find yourself engaged in, take time to ask yourself: How much of this is founded on a desire to do God's will, and how much is my self-centered concern for my own well-being?

113. Paul planted it, Apollos tended it, and God prospered it (see 1 Corinthians 3:6).

114. If there is no resurrection and no supernatural life to be looked for, we Christians are the most unfortunate people in the world.

115. You proclaim that all you do is "for God and for the Church." Very well. But can you stand in his presence and honestly say that you are working completely for him? God must truly be the essential object of all your activities and you should be ashamed to admit any other motive.

116. If you have dedicated your life to the service of God, why do you still waste time comparing yourself with others,

complaining constantly about this or that circumstance? Do you regret serving God because of some of the "losses" which you have suffered?

117. When the seventy-two disciples returned rejoicing over the wonders for which they had been able to be the instruments and expecting, no doubt, commendation, Jesus gave them the mild rejoinder: "Do not rejoice in this, that the spirits are subject to you, but rejoice that your names are written in heaven" (Luke 10:20). We should likewise rejoice more in the eternal life which awaits us than any miracles we should come across in the present.

Seven: Prayer

My vocation is to pray.

118. Action without prayer is useless in the eyes of God—otherwise, a robot would be worth more than you.

119. In our lives, prayer must come first, sacrifice second, then (and only then) in the third place is activity.

120. As a lightbulb brightens when connected to a generator, so are you when you are joined in communication with God in prayer. Prayer is the foundation of the spiritual life.

121. You believe that prayer is all-powerful, don't you? Consider our Lord's words: "Ask, and it will be given you; seek, and you will find; knock and it will be opened to you" (Luke 11:9). Is there a more certain guarantee than this?

122. Prayer is the only secret of nurturing the Christian life. Should there be someone who does not pray, even if he should perform a miracle, do not believe in him.

123. Pray always and everywhere. Jesus himself instructs us on the necessity of praying always (see Luke 18:1) so that we "may not enter into temptation" (Matthew 26:41).

124. "Where two or three are gathered in my name, there am I in the midst of them" (Matthew 18:20). These words of the Lord are especially fulfilled in those many communities which, deprived of a priest, still pray together. They still organize themselves to pray in community and hold firmly to this practice despite their difficulties and isolation.

125. Are you surprised that many people today have lost the grace of God, lost their faith, or have turned against the Church? While many causes could be proposed for this sad phenomenon, the explanation is simple enough: These people have stopped praying.

126. Do not neglect your oral prayers. When the apostles asked Jesus, "Lord, teach us to pray" (Luke 11:1), he responded by giving them the Our Father—that is, an oral prayer.

127. While you are taught to recite certain prayers in order to help you to pray, prayer itself is actually an encounter and conversation between the Father and his children. "When you pray,

go into your room and shut the door and pray to your Father who is in secret. Then your Father, who sees in secret, will reward you" (Matthew 6:6). There is no need to be formal; simply pray from your heart, speaking as a child would to its father.

128. The prayers of the liturgy are especially pleasing to God because they are drawn from his Word in the Bible or from the official prayer of the Church, which is the Mystical Body of Christ. Use a missal, psalter, or approved prayer book to help your prayers.

129. It is not without foundation that I assert that prayer is of the utmost importance. Jesus himself declared, "Mary has chosen the good portion which shall not be taken away from her" (Luke 10:42). So indeed, since as she sat at the Lord's feet and listened lovingly to his words, Mary had in him all that we now have in the Holy Eucharist, the Bible, and the whole of liturgical prayer.

130. You seek a friend who will comfort you and ease your loneliness. Why not look for the friend who will never let you down and who will be with you always, no matter where you are?

131. A seemingly holy person who does not pray is no saint. Watch closely and see; the facade will crumble before long.

132. You can always judge a person's apostolic effectiveness by looking at his prayer life.

133. If you are not a person of prayer, no one will believe that you work for God alone.

134. Why is there a crisis in the Church? It is because people do not take prayer seriously anymore.

135. Prayer should be as fervent as the prayer of the Virgin Mary and the apostles in the Upper Room awaiting the Holy Spirit, as trusting in the Father as that of Jesus in the Garden of Olives, as resolute as that of Moses when he stretched out his arms on the mountain during the battle, and as confident in the mercy of God as that of the good thief at Calvary.

136. "Man shall not live by bread alone but by every word that proceeds from the mouth of God" (Matthew 4:4)—that is, the Holy Eucharist, the Bible, and liturgical prayer. Without these, there can be no spiritual life.

137. Prayer on the lips of an unbaptized person is a genuine sign of the beginnings of faith.

138. The spirit of prayer can be compared to a furnace burning in your apostolic soul. If you wish to feed the fire, you must stir up the logs of sacrifice and recollection as well as the smaller sticks of frequent aspirations and secret acts of self-denial.

139. Even if you do not even utter one word, God understands your heart completely. Look at the example of the woman who was suffering from the hemorrhage (see Matthew 9:20–22). As

soon as she touched the hem of our Lord's cloak in faith, she was cured instantly without so much as a word said.

140. As a sinner, you are afraid to stand in the presence of God. But the words of the Church's liturgical prayer—"through Jesus Christ our Lord"—should reassure you. How could you think that all the sufferings of Jesus and all the good works of his mother and the saints would not be sufficient to encompass your little prayers?

141. Do you think that children are not yet able and that the sick are no longer able to do anything for the Church? No, not at all. After the official prayer of the Church, the prayers of children and the sick are most pleasing to God. Remember this and remind children and the sick of this great truth.

142. Your time of prayer is your period of intimacy with God, who is your Father. It is a time for the heart, not the head. Do not rack your brains or scratch your head as to how you should appear before God.

143. There are many places in the world where, deprived of priests, the laity have been able to keep alive the faith for decades. Their secret? Families which pray together.

144. Without forgetting the realities within and around you, your prayers should nevertheless include everyone, and your heart should encompass the world.

145. Spiritual books have helped many people to become saints. They are the oil that fuels the furnace of prayer.

146. In a sense, consecrated souls should declare on their identity cards, "Occupation: Prayer." For while others are attending to the various other tasks in the world, these individuals are called upon by the world to assume the role of representative and to intercede for it.

147. It was not out of laziness that Mary sat quietly at the Lord's feet; the Gospels do not canonize lazy people. Rather, she chose the better part by electing to listen to our Lord and to allow his words to enter her heart and soul and—by operating in and with her—to transform her. Could anything have been more active than that renewal, that inner transformation?

Eight: Sacrifice

Sacrifice is the proof of love.

148. Sacrifice and contemplative prayer go hand in hand. If you do not practice self-sacrifice, do not complain that your prayer has grown cold.

149. You will have to make many sacrifices in order to live peacefully and charitably with other people who differ from you politically, socially, or ideologically. Take for your example Jesus himself. He who is God had to live among sinful human beings—that was thirty-three years of continual sacrifice.

150. If someone torments you, you can adopt one of two attitudes: "This person is hurting me" or "This person is sanctifying me."

151. When everyone else would be saying, "This person is a nuisance," you should say, "This person is the instrument which God is using to transform me."

152. People venerate those holy persons who have been privileged to bear on their own bodies the stigmata, that is, the five wounds of Jesus. Yet all true Christians impress Christ's wounds on their body through their personal sacrifices.

153. You say that you have not been able to offer any sacrifices to God, yet you reject so many opportunities when they are presented. For example, be happy and joyful when someone ridicules you or tries to provoke you; be silent in the face of false accusations or outright persecution; show love to a friend who has betrayed you; utter no words in retaliation. Every single moment is full of opportunities for self-sacrifice.

154. Do not sacrifice in the manner of Pharisees, but sacrifice in the spirit of the Gospels.

155. A person who truly loves will sacrifice himself all the time and will never utter a word about it.

156. If you have "not had the opportunity to sacrifice," it is a sign that you still have not learned to love God.

157. If there is no sacrifice, there will be no holiness. You must deny yourself and take up your cross before you are able to follow Jesus. Self-denial is the prerequisite of holiness.

158. You must sacrifice yourself, not other people.

159. For the sake of love, we should be prepared to sacrifice anything, since "I do as the Father has commanded me, so that the world may know that I love the Father. Rise, let us go hence" (John 14:31).

160. If you do not practice external sacrifice, the chances are that you do not practice interior sacrifice either. Mortification of the senses is most important. Remember, David fell because he did not keep his eyes from wandering.

161. Jesus "having loved his own who were in the world, loved them to the end" (John 13:1), even the end on the Cross. Your sacrifice must be complete: It must be a total holocaust if you are truly to love to the end.

162. Let go of what separates you from the Lord. Recall his words: "Better that you lose one of your members than that your whole body be thrown into hell" (Matthew 5:30).

163. God often sends crosses to those he loves, but such people whom God loves in this special way are few in number since too many people are unwilling to suffer and sacrifice.

164. If you fail to sacrifice in small things, you will surrender when confronted with the need for big sacrifices.

165. As an incentive for yourself, always define an intention when you prepare to make a sacrifice; for example, offer your sacrifice for the intention of saving a soul, strength for some sick or lonely person, or of relief for a particular church which may be suffering obstacles or difficulties.

166. The way you begin the day is of the greatest importance. Rise up eagerly each morning, and this enthusiasm will help to carry you throughout the day.

167. Do not be afraid. Read the Acts of the Apostles: Enduring hunger and thirst, suffering poverty, robberies, beatings, shipwreck, false accusations, imprisonment, and even death (see 2 Corinthians 11:24–7) was their lot in life. If you are afraid, you can never be an apostle.

168. If you practice self-discipline by means of sacrifice, your soul and body will become like two friends who are united and invincible. But if you cannot discipline yourself, your soul and your body will become two enemies in constant conflict, tearing you apart forever.

169. You should be tolerant toward the faults and imperfections of others while remaining always strict toward your own.

170. There are some people who make sacrifices, but then want everyone else to know about it. There are other people who never make sacrifices, but would have everyone else believe that

they do. Then there are still others who frequently practice sacrifice and mortification, but do not want anyone to know about it.

171. In a solemn pilgrimage in which hundreds or even thousands of people take part, everybody wants to carry the cross at the head of the procession. But in the pilgrimage of everyday life, how many are prepared to carry their own crosses? It is indeed difficult to be an unsung hero.

172. The choice is between holiness or sinfulness. In many instances, the choice is the result of victory or defeat in one moment requiring sacrifice.

173. The profession of faith, the Creed, should sharpen our appreciation of the sacrifice of our Lord: He was "incarnate of the Virgin Mary . . . crucified under Pontius Pilate, he suffered death and was buried." His sacrifice was that of an entire lifetime, a sacrifice in a complete holocaust.

174. You should be able to sacrifice your life, your whole existence, readily because of the overwhelming hope we have in Jesus Christ who "rose again on the third day in accordance with the Scriptures . . . ascended into heaven and is seated at the right hand of the Father . . . will come again in glory . . . and his kingdom will have no end."

175. Do not go about thinking that you are the only person making sacrifices. Look at all the humanity around you: from small

children to old women who have sacrificed everything to rear good children and grandchildren. You should be ashamed of yourself! You would be amazed to know that there are some people who are very poor and unsightly, but that below their tatters lie real heroes and heroines.

Nine: The Heart

Never let your heart grow old.

176. Do not give your heart to God and then look for the heart of another to fill the apparent void. Neither God nor you is a surgeon working on heart transplants.

177. The older saints get, the younger their hearts become.

178. Do not let your heart grow old with the passing of time. Love with a love which daily grows ever more intense, ever more new, ever more pure—that is, with the love which God pours into your heart.

179. Why are you so hesitant? If you are bound by any chain, even if it be of gold, cut yourself loose so that you can be free to progress down this road. Our Lord is waiting to welcome you at the end of your journey.

180. Every time you fall, you keep saying, "Oh, if only I had made a stronger resolution in the beginning!" I hope you do not keep having these belated regrets.

181. You feel that your heart is wavering. Well, this need not be a cause for fear. The saints had the same feeling, but then turned it round and used it—with God's grace and their own efforts—to become saints.

182. You offer God a heart which all sorts of disorderly things are struggling to possess. How can you expect God to accept such a heart?

183. How can you expect to be given the love of our Lord's heart when all you will give him is that crumpled heart of yours?

184. You say that "friendship keeps me going." But consider this: If you are making no progress on your spiritual journey, it may be because such friendship is really a burden crushing you.

185. You peddle your heart to all comers. Then, when you find no buyers, you take it as an offering to our Lord. Don't you think he can see through all this?

186. The Lord asks you to give yourself totally, not halfheartedly, to him.

187. If you will give up everything, you will win everything.

Remember, Jesus himself said, "I, when I am lifted up from the earth, will draw all men to myself" (John 12:32).

188. Do not think that because you give everything up your heart will be cold or your life will be lonely or you will not be attractive. On the contrary, your heart will shine forth with the light and warmth of the Sacred Heart of Jesus. Just look at the power of attraction which the saints have had through the centuries.

189. The saints gave up everything, but the whole world followed them wherever they went, no matter how isolated or deserted the place. Look at the example of St. John Vianney or Padre Pio.

190. You are not willing to follow the will of God, yet you allow other people to enslave you.

191. Heart or duty: Which would you choose if you had to? Choose duty and then carry it out with all your heart.

192. To be motivated by one's emotions to labor in the apostolate may appear to be very good, but upon closer examination we find that before long emotions will prevail over the apostle.

193. Many frivolous attachments chain you and prevent you from rising to better things.

194. What is important is not the number of your activities, but the degree of love which transforms them.

Ten: Fortitude

*Resolve to be steeped in one book, the Gospel,
and to be inspired by one ideal, the life of Jesus Christ.*

195. God has given you the gift of life. He has also given you the freedom to make that life holy and wonderfully effective, or to misuse it so as to stunt that life, betraying God's gift and turning it to evil.

196. Selfish people avoid responsibility and sacrifice, and shy away from occasions where they might tire themselves out. These people seek to create their own heaven in this world, but they will end by losing the paradise and happiness which lasts for all eternity.

197. The Christian regards everyone in the world as his brothers and sisters and is as concerned about their work as if it were his own. The selfish person, on the other hand, regards everyone

else as rungs on a ladder to be climbed for his own advancement. Such a person knows only "my work" and "my possessions."

198. To exploit people in order to advance your personal interests is unworthy of a leader. You will be a worthy leader only if you do not distance yourself from the people, but rather if you mix with them and are even willing to risk your life for their sake.

199. Do not regard cowardice as prudence. It is because so many people have this kind of "wisdom" that darkness prevails in so many situations.

200. A Christian is never self-satisfied. Self-satisfaction is a wall which separates one from God, from other people, and from all creation.

201. The great-hearted person does not boast; rather he or she has a spirit of self-sacrifice. Such a person is like the lump of sugar or grain of salt which, when dissolved, adds flavor to food.

202. A great-hearted person is straightforward and neither pries into the affairs of others nor acts deviously when dealing with them.

203. If you are a Christian, you know your limitations and do not go about interfering in other people's business.

204. Know when to keep quiet. Too much idle talk without

thought of the consequences gives rise to disharmony. Useless words are the devil's instrument to undermine charity.

205. Do not be inquisitive about the affairs of others. Concentrate on knowing yourself first.

206. The habit of criticizing others is one of the greatest obstacles to the growth of a spiritual life. Blaming others serves only to irritate them and cultivates bitterness in your own heart.

207. Never permit failures, trials, or sufferings to be an occasion for blaming others.

208. *Laissez-faire* is a word in the dictionary of cowards, those lazy persons who refuse to struggle because they have already accepted defeat.

209. Avoid false humility. It is necessary to be ambitious in the pursuit of knowledge and the desire to act and take risks. Just remember, however, that these things are for God and his Church.

210. Refrain from violent arguments which lead to a loss of perspective. Passion is like a dark cloud which blocks out God's light.

211. Friction with other people is a normal part of life. The only society without friction is the kingdom of heaven. By means of friction, a stone can become smoother, rounder, cleaner, and more beautiful.

212. Do not allow yourself to become contaminated with superficiality. This disease causes the gradual death of the will. Its symptoms are a constant changing of opinion or activity. To safeguard yourself against this malady, do not accumulate a stockpile of projects which will never be finished.

213. Superficial people are like dancing puppets, which in reality go nowhere and do nothing. This very day is when you must put your plans into action. Do not put things off until later.

214. God created you to lead others, and not to be led about like a sheep with the rest of the flock. To lead means to urge and encourage, to carry others along with you.

215. All the small things which you do are very important; do not despise them because they are small. If you conquer yourself in the small things, you will train your will to be rock solid and truly become master of yourself.

216. Before you say anything, consider the way you will say it: Your message will be heard only if you speak with charity and courtesy. The same message, spoken by two different people in two different ways, always produces two different results.

217. Do not browbeat or nag someone who has made a mistake. Wait patiently. You will achieve more good by speaking gently and with good will than by an outburst of abuse. By so acting, you will both make your point and control your temper.

218. Resolve to do what needs to be done neither with fear nor with hesitation. Take courage and be full of hope; trust in God and in your own courage.

219. When confronted by obstacles, stand firm as a rock; the grace of God will never be lacking. And even if you must temporarily curtail your activities, do not worry. After all, the work you do is more God's work than your own.

220. Time and energy belong to God. Do not squander them on unimportant obstacles. The ocean is full of waves, yet the well-built boat will continue on its way, gliding over the waters and ignoring the waves.

221. Do not allow yourself to become agitated and angry. Remain calm and self-composed. Agitation and anger offend God, irritate those around you, and make you unhappy as well. So what is their use if they leave you only with regrets once the incident has passed?

222. Do not say: "I was made like this; I can't change." No, we are talking about your faults and imperfections. You must be mature, you must become a true child of God; continuing in these faults and imperfections will prevent you becoming one.

223. Turn your back on those small-minded people who constantly whisper in your ear, "You are mad to put up with such a miserable life!" Remember how Jesus dismissed Peter with the

words, "Get behind me, Satan! You are a hindrance to me; for you are not on the side of God, but of men" (Matthew 16:23).

224. You should acquire the habit of being able to refuse, of knowing how to say no.

225. Do not be particular or parochial in regard to where or with whom you live and work, but open wide your heart so that all humanity may find a place there. Otherwise, you may be Christian in name, but not in reality.

226. Illumine your life with the virtues of faith and charity. Set fire to the world with the flame God has ignited in your heart.

227. Always act in such a way that your thoughts, words, and deeds will lead others to conclude, "This person is steeped in one book, the Gospel, and inspired by one ideal, the life of Jesus Christ."

228. Be serious and constant. Your exterior demeanor should reflect the interior life of your soul—that is, your peace of soul and self-control, rather than childish fear.

229. When the father of Bernadette Soubirous took her to the convent she was to enter, he laid down one condition: "Don't force my daughter to eat cheese—it would kill her." Thereafter, day after day for seven long years, Bernadette struggled at meals: "I must eat the cheese . . . I can't eat it . . .

I must eat the cheese . . ." Eventually she triumphed over herself, and such was her courage that she could eat it. That fortitude, evidenced in such small things, was what made her a saint.

Eleven: The Presence of God

If God is present, your life is no longer lonely.

230. Put your hand over your heart often and tell yourself: "God is living with me and in me." Little by little, God will give you a taste of that happiness which his presence brings.

231. "Where is God? God is in heaven." There is something missing when we teach small children this stock reply in their catechisms. We should add, "God is living in me." That answer is far more accurate and will bring these little ones greater happiness, inviting them into a relationship with him.

232. The several thousand patients in the House of St. Joseph Cottolengo have a special expression on their faces, for from time to time a gentle voice can be heard over the public address system repeating a simple phrase: "God is here at our side!"

233. The pealing of the church bell or the sight of its tower should be a reminder to you that God is in the tabernacle nearby. Raise your heart, then, to that place to love and worship him.

234. God's presence in you is not just a pious idea; it is a reality. God our Father is at your side with all his power and love. He is the Father who persuades, counsels, calls, admonishes, forgives, and loves you always.

235. Jesus should be everything to you: the object of all your desires, the reason behind all of your decisions, the motivation of all your emotions, and the model for all your actions.

236. Think for a moment of the presence of a very loving or inspiring person—perhaps of a gentle, caring mother or even an important dignitary—who affirms you, makes you feel self-confident, reassures you. All the love, kindness, and honor which this person's presence gives you is nothing compared to that which is conferred by the presence of God. God's presence exceeds all others to such a degree that a million times the distance from the earth to the sun would not begin to express its infinite superiority.

237. Why do some Christians complain that they are lonely? Where is their Christ?

238. Consider the greeting of the angel Gabriel—"Hail, full of grace, the Lord is with you!" (Luke 1:28)—and that of the

Church—"The Lord be with you." Are not these salutations full of profound significance, capable of changing your life?

239. In your relationship with God, your conscientious rectitude of intention may be sufficient. However, in dealing with other people, you also need to have prudence because their eyes cannot penetrate your conscience.

240. Ask our mother Mary to lead you to Jesus, and you will know what it is to live by his side.

241. The presence of God at your side is not a matter of feelings. Rather, God takes possession of you, guiding, loving, and consoling you.

242. Live at God's side and you will assuredly become a saint, since heaven is nothing other than the presence of God.

243. Confide frequently in Mary, the beloved Mother of God. This is most pleasing to God who is present in your heart.

244. Since the Blessed Trinity lives in you, you are the temple of God, the dwelling place which is also the holocaust, the word of endless praise, the flower of great beauty which is offered up.

245. Why are you so eager to build churches of wood and stone, and yet remain unwilling to transform your soul into a temple of God?

246. Do not be concerned about whether you live in a beautiful palace or an ugly hut, so long as you make your home an abode of love. Then it will become heaven, because God will be there.

Twelve: The Church

One Body: the Church
One leader: the Holy Father
One hope: "That all may be one" (John 17:21).

247. Whenever anyone expressed concern about the sufferings or the fatigues of labor which he had to endure, Pope Paul VI would always reply, "For the Church! For the Church." You should try to follow his example and have the Church as your *raison d'etre*.

248. Those who truly love the Church do not seek to destroy it.

249. "I tell you, you are Peter, and on this rock I will build my church, and the powers of death shall not prevail against it" (Matthew 16:18). The twenty centuries which have come and gone since Jesus made that promise to Peter have seen many ups and downs, many crises for the Church. There have been

attacks from within as well as without. Many times, the Church has found herself in desperate situations. Nevertheless, the Church continues to stand firm because it is the Church of God, not just another human institution.

250. "We believe in one, holy, catholic and apostolic Church." We have but one faith; we know the same happiness; we share a common determination!

251. Do not be surprised when you see people seeking to destroy the Church. They would like to kill Christ again, but since they cannot do so, they seek to destroy the Church, his Mystical Body.

252. There are many people who criticize the Vatican bureaucracy. I would agree with them that the Roman Curia is not always perfect. However, I would ask them whether the government of their own countries is any better. Besides, one must distinguish between the Curia, which is just a human organization, and the Church itself, the Mystical Body of Christ.

253. Love the Church, obey the Church, be loyal to the Church, pray for the Church.

254. Some people are constantly criticizing "the Church"; they find the Curia too slow, the church buildings too ornate, the liturgy too elaborate. These people only betray their distorted idea of the Church—the Curia, buildings, and ceremonies are not the Church. The Church is the entire pilgrim people of God advancing toward the kingdom of heaven.

255. It is necessary to distinguish between questions of theology and history. The Pope may not necessarily be the most humanly capable person in the Church, but he is the one chosen by God to exercise authority over the Church in his name. He is the one you must obey because it is to him that God has given the keys of the kingdom of heaven.

256. The liturgy of the Church is not aimed at merely personal salvation or edification. It unites us with the entire people of God throughout the world because it unites us with Christ our Head and with his vicar on earth, the pope. Humankind is set free and united by the constant memorial of the life, death, and resurrection of Christ. Without this unity, we would be like a branch of the grapevine which is severed from its stem, we would be Catholic in name only.

257. Do not say that the Church has "been renewed"—it is continuously being renewed.

258. The Church was born on the cross, and thus it grows by renewing the passion of Jesus until the end of time. If you put your trust in money, diplomacy, power, influence, or campaigns of any kind, you will be sadly misled.

259. You claim that you would never turn against the Church, but that you only oppose the representatives of the Church. If this is your belief, you are only playing the game of the Pharisees. They claimed never to oppose Yahweh, but killed those whom he sent. What absurd logic!

260. You attack "structure," but why do you then insist on having organizations of all kinds and appointing numerous people to an endless stream of newly created committees and subcommittees? You are like the people who ridicule the practice of writing abbreviations—UNO, UNESCO, etc.— and then proceed to set up AAA (an Association Against Abbreviations). Your behavior is contradictory.

261. There are many kinds of Christians. There are the Christians who merely make use of the Church. There are those who are Christians in name only. There are the opportunists. And then there are those "honorary Christians" looking for status in society. However, the Lord accepts only those who are 100 percent Christian, those who accept him unconditionally and have "left everything and followed him" (Luke 5:11).

262. Naturally, no Christian sets out to betray the Church simply for the sake of betraying it. However, many are often led to do so when they experience one of three things:

1) financial or emotional problems
2) thwarted ambitions
3) threat of suffering or death

263. During the last two thousand years, the Church has been betrayed by apostles, popes, cardinals, bishops, priests, religious, and lay people—sometimes in small things, sometimes in the extraordinary "self-destruction" deplored by Pope Paul VI. Nevertheless, after each of these upheavals, the Church has

renewed itself and attained greater brilliance and strength. This is because the Church continues to live the mystery of the passion and resurrection.

264. There do exist within the Church today many imperfections and all too many bad examples. Nevertheless, the Church does enjoy God's promise of endurance and is thus a continuous miracle. However, this does not give you a license to expose all the faults for all to see whenever it suits you.

265. Be ready to sacrifice for the Church and through the Church.

266. "He who hears you, hears me, and he who rejects you, rejects me, and he who rejects me, rejects him who sent me" (Luke 10:16). Throughout your life, always keep this counsel impressed firmly on your heart. Respect those who represent the Church and who administer its Sacraments and Magisterium. God will bless you for this.

267. In the Church, everyone has a vocation, in fact a duty, to be holy. If you are not leading a life of holiness, do not presume to reform the Church. Remember that: "No one speaking by the Spirit of God ever says, 'Jesus be cursed!' and no one can say, 'Jesus is Lord' except by the Holy Spirit" (1 Corinthians 12:3).

268. You believe in the Church because it alone was established by Jesus Christ, and you thus suffer when you see the imperfections in the human face of the Church. You yourself, however,

share in the responsibility for these imperfections. You must strive to eradicate them and to bring about the will of God in the Church.

269. Before you criticize the Church as "irrelevant," read the encyclicals and other documents of the popes. You may be surprised to learn that they have dealt with every problem with deep insight. You will find that the policies of renewal were truly "radical" and that the spirit of Christianity (enlightened as it is by the Scriptures, the grace of God, and tradition) is really quite advanced. As Pope Pius XII noted, if we would only learn to put into practice just a small part of papal teaching, both the Church and the world would surely be transformed.

270. The Church belongs to young and old, intellectuals and laborers, rich and poor. The Church belongs to the yellow-skinned races, to the black people, and to those with white skins. It belongs to women as well as to men. The Church is the Church Universal, it accepts all without distinction. Discrimination and division have no place in the Church.

Thirteen: Faith

Light up the world with the flame of faith.

271. As you travel along the Road of Hope, you will need a light to guide you through those inevitable times of darkness and difficulty. That light will be the faith which the Church passed on to you on the day of your baptism.

272. Even if you face the most attractive of promises or are confronted with the most fearful of threats, you must remain steadfast in your confession: "I am a child of the Church. I am a descendant of the saints. I follow the faith which guides me."

273. In order to hold on firmly to your faith, you must choose the Road of Hope followed by the disciples of Christ and not the road to death offered by the world.

274. Many people today repeatedly assert, "I have the faith, I still have the faith." Perhaps they really do, but all too often their daily lives are at variance with the faith they profess with their lips. All too few live in complete accord with faith.

275. A thorough examination of your actions and reactions is sufficient to indicate whether yours is a living, vibrant faith or merely another label.

276. Jesus clearly promised that we would be able to accomplish great things with ease if only we have faith. Why? Because it is not we, but God himself who performs the actions.

277. We do not believe in a God who is distant or vague. Rather, we profess with Peter, "You are the Christ, the Son of the living God" (Matthew 16:16), while knowing with John that, "He who does not love does not know God; for God is love" (1 John 4:8).

278. If you only have faith, you will have everything and will even be able to work great wonders. Remember: "Your faith has saved you" (Luke 7:50).

279. In the Gospels, the apostles humbly relate their weakness of faith so that we may believe more strongly.

280. Do not be satisfied with a merely formal and theoretical faith. Rather let your faith be living, genuine, loving, and loyal.

281. There is no peace which can compare with the confidence which comes from living as a member of the Church. For in the bosom of the Church all anxiety is calmed and the heart is filled with hope.

282. Imitate the apostles in praying, "Increase our faith" (Luke 17:5).

283. Faith is the unconditional acceptance of Jesus Christ as Lord and the determination to live and die with him.

284. Our God is almighty and everlasting. If you will only believe in him, you will be able to do extraordinary things just as Jesus did. In fact, as he has promised, you will do even greater things.

285. Do not make false pretenses in order to avoid dangers and difficulties. Remember the words of Eleazer, who could have easily escaped martyrdom by a simply pretending to violate the law: "'Such pretense is not worthy of our time of life,' he said, 'lest many of the young should suppose that Eleazar in his ninetieth year has gone over to an alien religion, and through my pretense, for the sake of living a brief moment longer, they should be led astray because of me, while I defile and disgrace my old age. For even if for the present I should avoid the punishment of men, yet whether I live or die I shall not escape the hands of the Almighty'" (2 Maccabees 6:24–26).

286. Even though you may not be forced to deny our Lord explicitly, you may come under pressure to act in opposition to his

teaching and will be tempted to do so, thinking, *I still preserve my faith inside*. Do not be so deceived; a faith that recoils from death, suffering, or hardships will surely die.

287. Have the courage to live the life of faith every day. Imitate the martyrs who courageously held steadfast in their faith.

288. As Christians, we must believe above all else that we are redeemed, forgiven, and infinitely loved by God. Our Lord is not a Savior who forces us to love and reverence him, but rather he is the Savior we should love freely without reservation.

289. Christians should recognize the supremacy of God, not because he is almighty, but because he is all-loving.

290. The redemption of the human race should not be thought of in terms of action or practice, but in terms of mystery—the mystery of the death and resurrection of the Lord Jesus.

Fourteen: The Apostle

The apostle makes present again the life of Jesus.

291. Being an apostle requires being like the apostles. Therefore, if you wish to be an apostle reflect on the Acts of the Apostles and strive to understand them.

292. In the early Church, an apostle was commonly described as one with Christ in his heart, in his speech, in his actions—that is, in his whole demeanor—and even in his body. In short, an apostle was one who was filled with Christ and radiated him to others.

293. Apostolic work involves the sanctification of the environment by those in the midst of it. The worker is the apostle of the workers, the student is the apostle of the students, the soldier is the apostle of the soldiers.

294. "He who endures to the end will be saved" (Matthew 10:22). There will be more rejoicing in hell over the fall of one apostle than over the fall of a host of any others. Let us therefore pray for and support one another.

295. Good works by themselves do not make an apostle. The true apostle does good works because they are part of God's work.

296. Granted we live in a different period from that of the apostles, with different needs which demand different approaches in the apostolate. Nevertheless, Christ did give this assurance: "Lo, I am with you always, to the close of the age" (Matthew 28:20). He is still with the Church and continues to give it a new Pentecost.

297. Work away at your apostolate with your entire heart and soul. However, be prepared to share your energies with everyone and to cooperate with those less capable than yourself. Do not monopolize everything as if nothing could be done without you.

298. There are some things which you may yearn to do, but are unable to accomplish. These desires are often more meritorious, more pleasing to God, than all the results which give you self-satisfaction.

299. When you encounter difficulties, do not allow yourself to be discouraged. Simply ask yourself: "Is this God's work or mine? Is God doing this or am I?"

300. Before you complain about someone, ask yourself: "Is my salt still sharp to the taste? Is my lamp still burning bright?"

301. In dealing with other people, it may sometimes be necessary to be selective. However, it is never necessary to criticize, distrust, or despise others. The disciples Jesus chose to build his Church were filled with imperfections, but he asked them only to be childlike and to follow him loyally.

302. To the extent to which you permit your ego to grow, to that same extent your apostolic work will become a failure. The more you let your ego die, the more your apostolate will flourish.

303. Be ready to sacrifice those comforts which are unbecoming to a true apostle. Do not create "needs" that are not really necessities.

304. Do not allow yourself to become a person of many words and little action. On the other hand, do not become strong in action, but weak in prayer. Do not accept freely yet give sparingly. Do not be easy on yourself while being strict with others.

305. The light of your apostolic activities must shine out until the darkness around it is overcome and the entire world is immersed in the light of Christ. Be an apostle to apostles.

306. No one has a monopoly of representing God in their apostolate. When the apostles complained to Jesus, "Teacher, we saw a man casting out demons in your name, and we forbade him,

because he was not following us," he replied, "He that is not against us is for us" (Mark 9:38, 40).

307. You become annoyed when other apostles do not follow your style. While it is true that there must be unity, it is likewise true that there can be many facets to this unity.

308. No two saints are alike, just as no two stars in the sky are alike. Yet all the saints are alike in one regard: They each reflect some aspect of the life of Jesus.

309. One of the most important tasks in the apostolate is to choose and train zealous co-workers. A famous leader once said, "Give me three hundred brave soldiers and I will rule until death." Jesus did better: He chose twelve men and built a Church to last until the end of time.

310. There is no need to have any special status or position before you can begin your work as an apostle. Do not feel discouraged because of your low status or because of the high status of others. After all, are you working for God or for status?

311. The apostle may have one position today and another tomorrow, but he will feel neither loss nor gain. He is conscious of only one thing: "The Son of Man come not to be served but to serve, and to give his life as a ransom for many" (Matthew 20:28).

312. You are downcast because of a loss of position or because

you were not placed where you want to be. Why do you think only in terms of worldly calculations?

313. When you accept the responsibility of being an apostle, you indicate a readiness also to accept martyrdom with all the love and perseverance of Peter and John—whenever, however, and from whoever it is offered. Remember, they "left the presence of the council, rejoicing that they were counted worthy to suffer dishonor for the name" (Acts 5:41).

314. The most dangerous enemy of apostolic work is the enemy within. It was Judas, the treasurer of the Twelve, who betrayed Jesus.

315. The greatest danger to your apostolic work will not be an external enemy or one of your rivals. Rather, it will be the enemy within yourself. Unless you are vigilant, you may find yourself a double agent working for both sides, God and the devil.

316. An apostle respects higher authority even when he could easily prove the unsuitability of a superior's order. In the presence of others, he will always treat his superiors with respect. Disobedience and duplicity are inexcusable in an apostle.

317. If you display an air of self-satisfaction, you will repel everyone and no one will believe that your works are under the guidance of the Holy Spirit.

318. If you fight the enemy on all sides, and yet have no charity, all

your exertions will come to nothing. Rather, you will be like the man who bought colored lamps and strung them throughout a village which had no electrical generator. When the night came and the village remained pitch black, the villagers learned the truth: The man's lamps could decorate, but could not light up anything.

319. If you are insulted, persecuted, and driven from one town after another, this is a sign that God loves you and that he has chosen you to be a true apostle. Recall that: "If you were of the world, the world would love its own; but because you are not of the world, but I chose you out of the world, therefore the world hates you. Remember the word that I said to you, 'A servant is not greater than his master.' If they persecuted me, they will persecute you; if they kept my word, they will keep yours also" (John 15:19–20).

320. The aim of apostolic work is to bring others into the one Church, and not to establish partisan or national churches. Even if such attempts were not schismatic, they would be nevertheless a great hindrance to the mission of the Church.

321. An apostle who suffers (even when he is neither preaching nor performing any great works) can quietly offer himself as a sacrifice for others. Thus, while Jesus was dying on the cross, his mother was suffering quietly at its foot.

322. There are many different ways of being an apostle. Being one by means of sacrifice is like being a grain of rice which is buried in the ground to decay in order that it may give birth to many other grains which will feed mankind.

Then an apostle affects other people by his witness and way of life. Mere words, regardless of how eloquent and inviting they may be, will not convince others. Remember, people may be impressed with someone's photograph or recording. But if they have him present in flesh and bones, if they see his whole life—or better yet, that of his entire family or community—lived according to one ideal, what a persuasive force that witness would have!

323. Then there is personal contact. "Did not our hearts burn within us while he talked to us on the road, while he opened to us the scriptures?" (Luke 24:32). Regard every contact as an apostolic encounter.

324. Some exercise their apostolate by counseling others. They help those who are in crisis by opening new horizons for them, helping them to appreciate their own abilities and to hear the call of faith. These apostles bring hope to lives which are almost shattered. There would be fewer stories of drug overdoses, suicides, and the like if only there were more people like these apostles.

325. There are also apostles of the dinner table. A meal may be an ordinary, everyday event, but it was different when Jesus ate at the houses of Mary and Martha, Zacchaeus, and Simon Peter. His presence was salvific: "Today salvation has come to this house" (Luke 19:9).

326. Correspondence can also be the work of the apostle. When Paul was in prison, he had no modern conveniences—typewriters,

word processors, or photocopiers. Yet he wrote letters to Christian communities which in turn copied them for still other communities. In this way, Paul held on to the faith and helped to build it up in the early Church.

327. Women are called to be effective apostles. Look at Mary and Salome who followed Jesus and assisted him. St. Paul had many women fellow-workers in his apostolate; for example: "Greet these workers in the Lord, Tryphaenea and Tryphosa" (Romans 16:12).

328. From the very earliest times, courageous children have been apostles. Young St. Tarcisius carried the sacrament to many before suffering martyrdom. Remember the words of the Lord: "Let the children come to me, do not hinder them" (Mark 10:14).

329. The contemporary struggles by women for recognition in the Church should not be necessary. The Apostles gave women recognized status as collaborators in the work of the early Church.

330. Do not have doubts about yourself or others. Fishermen like Peter and tax collectors like Matthew have become great apostles by following the Lord's call: "Follow me and I will make you fishers of men" (Matthew 4:19). By yourself you cannot accomplish this; it is the work of the Lord.

331. Prepare your heart to receive and carry out the Church's mission of evangelization.

332. In times past, whenever there were rare spices or hidden treasures to be found, people would risk their lives to search them out. Today, countries will destroy each other to control petroleum, uranium, or other precious minerals. Yet where souls are concerned, few are found who are eager to search for them!

333. Some people do not take it seriously when they are told that lay people have a charism from the Holy Spirit. These same people find it unthinkable that the laity are also priests, prophets, and kings. How many laypeople are conscious of the reality that they have been called and are needed by God? How many are proud and grateful for having been made children of God by baptism and his soldiers and witnesses by confirmation?

334. This is the era of the laity. Thus, if we fail to mobilize all the strengths and talents of the people of God, if we do not encourage them to become aware of and active in their apostolic role, there will still be vast areas of modern society untouched by the message of the gospel.

335. The secret of the apostolate in our time is the lay apostle.

336. Just as seminary training is essential for a priest, an initial period of formation is absolutely necessary for any lay apostle.

337. A parish which invested in training just five authentic lay apostles would be assured of at least thirty or forty years of loyal service, right up to death. How much potential we leave unseen and untapped in the kingdom of God!

338. Do not be so enthusiastic about large numbers. Large numbers of people eventually become disparate and difficult to organize. On the other hand, look at the effectiveness of the political cadres: It only requires one party cadre to stir up and mobilize a mob of people. The well-trained party cadre is the heart and mind, the very backbone, of mass revolutionary movements.

339. Take the example of the secular institutes—new solutions for the challenges of a new era. They are truly a special grace which God has granted us in these times to promote a lay spirituality. The popes foresaw these developments decades before they were realized.

340. The role of the apostle in our time is to be in the midst of the world. Without being of the world, he must live for the world and be able to make use of its facilities.

341. As members of the Mystical Body, we are the minds to meditate and the eyes to look on the reality of the world, the ears to hear its cries and pleas, the arms to rescue and support; the feet to go to the suffering, the heart to bring compassion and love to those in need, the mouth to speak words of love and consolation. The Church is present in the world today through her apostles.

342. We often take water, light, and air for granted, but without them our world would die instantly. We are hardly conscious of the forces of nature working around us, but if they were to stop, we would cease to exist. Likewise, people often do not notice the humble presence and quiet labor of the apostle, but his absence is quickly felt in the emptiness of an environment which, without the light radiated by the apostle, becomes as cold as a grave.

Fifteen: The Eucharist

*Only an eternity of preparation and an eternity of thanksgiving
are sufficient to appreciate the value of one Eucharist.*

343. The Eucharist shapes Christians; Christians shape the Eucharist. The Eucharist shapes the Church; the Church shapes the Eucharist.

344. Those on the outside have great difficulty understanding why we keep going if day after day, the priest celebrates the selfsame Mass. They are partially correct. The Mass, regardless of who says it or where it is said, is always the same: It is the continuation of the one sacrifice of Calvary. They are mistaken, however, in their idea of its attraction. It is the power of the mystery which draws the people, for it is not the priest but Jesus himself who offers the sacrifice.

345. Some people claim that because they are "being sincere with God," they go to Mass only when they feel fervent. The truth of the matter, however, is that these people are not thinking of God when they go to Mass; they are there for self-satisfaction.

346. If you truly appreciate the value of the Mass, you will be present for its celebration no matter how far or difficult it may be to get to it. The greater the sacrifice involved, the more evident will be your love for God.

347. Have you ever met anyone who is more materially deprived than others simply on account of his or her spending too much time attending Mass?

348. People may go to the Eucharist together, but their sentiments differ vastly from one person to the next. Such was also the case at Calvary, as an analysis of those standing around the foot of the cross will show.

349. You want to know, "How can I most please God?" The answer is: Attend Mass. No prayer, no meeting, no ceremony, no action is comparable to the prayer and sacrifice of Jesus on the cross.

350. Saints are those who continue to live the Mass throughout their day.

351. We enjoy chatting for hours on end. When it comes to eating and drinking, the more time we take to dine leisurely, the greater

our pleasure. Some of us even derive satisfaction from gambling away the night. Why then are we in such a hurry to finish the Mass?

352. "The priest, because he represents Christ during the Mass, is the finest of tabernacles, the brightest of haloes, the most magnificent candlestick, and the most majestic church. A lukewarm priest in a cathedral attracts no one, but a holy priest in the shabbiest chapel in some remote place will bring crowds flocking to him" (Pere Chevrier).

353. A family that loves the Mass will be a holy family.

354. "An eternity of preparation and an eternity of thanksgiving alone suffice to appreciate one Holy Mass" (St. John Vianney).

355. The priest offers the Mass together with the Lord and when he distributes Holy Communion, he gives himself as well as the Lord to be food for all. In this way, the priest signifies that he is always totally available for others.

356. Our Lord's entire life was directed toward Calvary. Your entire life should be directed toward the Eucharist.

357. Each time you celebrate the Eucharist, you have the opportunity to stretch out your arms and nail yourself to the cross with Jesus and drink his bitter chalice to the dregs. There is no room for onlookers at the Eucharist.

358. I treasure that old-fashioned expression, "to offer Mass." After all, during the Mass, all the faithful are united with Christ and share in his eternal offering.

359. Do you want to glorify God?
Do you want to give thanks to God?
Do you want to pray to God?
Do you want to love God?
Do you want to save humanity?
Then take part in the Eucharist . . .
For it was only by means of the sacrifice of Calvary that the Lord accomplished all this.

360. A lamp can give no light if it has no oil. A car will not run on an empty fuel tank. The soul of the apostle will degenerate if it is not nourished with the Blessed Sacrament.

361. Just as the sun shines brightly shedding its light on the earth, so too does the Eucharist shine as the light for the spiritual life of human beings, and the source of peace among nations.

362. The Eucharist is meant to unite us into the one Mystical Body. To offer the Mass without love is a contradiction in terms.

363. If you lack everything or find yourself bereft of all possessions but still have the Eucharist, you should not be concerned. In fact, you still have everything, because you have the Lord of heaven here on earth with you.

364. If you are alone in some remote place or even if you find yourself in the darkness of prison: Take heart. Turn toward the altars of the world where the Lord Jesus Christ himself is offering sacrifice. Unite with the sacrifice of the Mass and make a spiritual communion with him. Your heart will then be filled to overflowing with all the consolation and courage you need.

365. How can you complain about exhausting themes for your meditation? The sacrifice of the Mass and the reception of Holy Communion are subjects with infinitely new dimensions of fruitful meditation.

366. The "Sunday Christian" will be unable to reform today's materialistic world. To live the Eucharist daily and constantly is the secret of bringing God into the world and leading the world to him.

367. Jesus began a true revolution on the cross. You must begin at his holy table and further this spiritual revolution to renew humanity.

368. Just as the drop of water poured into the chalice at Mass mingles completely with the wine, so should your life become one with that of Christ.

369. Your whole life should be nothing more and nothing less than a proclamation of the death of the Lord and a witness to his resurrection.

370. Jesus is the head of the Mystical Body which is the Church. Thus when we celebrate the Eucharist, we do so in communion with the Church. The Eucharistic Prayers declare that the offering made by the people of God is done "together with the Pope . . . and the Bishop." Only within this unity does the Mass have true meaning as an acceptable sacrifice.

371. The Mass makes the Church present to me and alive in me. In it, I hear the words of prophets and apostles, and of the Lord himself. I am united with the pope, my bishop, the hierarchy, the clergy, the religious, and the entire people of God on earth as well as in heaven—Mary, the saints, the holy souls—in order that through, with, and in Jesus Christ, I may offer all glory and honor to the Holy Trinity in the expectation of the Lord's glorious coming. How great is the happiness and hope which I thus receive from one Mass!

372. My whole life can be a continuous Eucharistic celebration: at times a penitential rite, at other times humbly praying to "Our Father" or joyfully chanting "Glory to God" and "Alleluia." Whatever it is, it is always an offering, a summons to prayer, and a proclamation of my faith in one God, in union with everyone through the love of the Holy Spirit and in communion with the Church throughout the world.

373. If you want to strengthen your faith, you must nourish yourself with the Eucharist, for this sacrament is the "mystery of faith" which strengthens it.

374. A seminarian is nourished by the Eucharist that he may become a golden grain of wheat which dies to be crushed into the bread of Christ's body given as food for the people of God.

375. For the fervent seminarian or priest, every day is a solemnity if Mass is offered. Each day calls for the solemnity of a high Mass, celebrated with ever-increasing fervor right until the end.

376. Every time you have the privilege of distributing the Eucharist to the people of God, remind yourself that with Christ you are giving the whole of your life, time, energy, talents, and possessions. This is to say that you are offering your own flesh and blood, together with the Body and Blood of the Lord, to be the nourishment of each and every person without distinction.

377. Offer yourself with Jesus every day, being ever prepared "to be poured out for many" (Matthew 26:28).

378. Every day, at the words of consecration, with all your heart and soul, renew the "new and everlasting covenant" between yourself and our Lord, by the mingling of your blood with his.

379. The Holy Eucharist conveys to our minds some understanding of the mystery of the kingdom of heaven hereafter and of the union of the people of God in this mystery. During this life, faith depends on the firmness of belief in the mystery of the kingdom of heaven. However, this faith cannot survive long in a Christian who tries to live without the Eucharist.

380. Your priestly life should center on an ardent love for the Mass. It should be central to your thoughts and actions. You should always be able to say with our Lord, "I have earnestly desired to eat this Passover with you" (Luke 22:15).

381. White, gold, green, red, violet, and black: The color of the vestments may change, but there is only one and the same Mass. You may commemorate many events—joy, hope, martyrdom, death—but whenever and wherever you do this, you do so "through him, with him, and in him."

382. Whenever you wear the distinctive clerical attire, symbolic of the charity within you, you give witness to the presence of God in the world. Yet now that you find such dress forbidden to you and you pass indistinguishable from others, how will you give witness to the Lord? But have no fear. Even though you are forced to change your external methods, you can still be recognized as one of Christ's disciples if you have love for your neighbor. On the other hand, if you have no love or if you have a poor disposition, no matter how much clerical garb you don or how eloquently you express yourself, no one will be convinced.

383. Remember that Jesus said, "Where two or three are gathered in my name, there am I in the midst of them" (Matthew 18:20); "Lo, I am with you always, to the close of the age" (Matthew 28:20); and "Do this in remembrance of me" (1 Corinthians 11:24). He laid down no material conditions with these promises. Therefore, avoid the two extremes: anxiety that there

is no place for the Lord to dwell and criticism of the work of building houses of God.

384. When people no longer respect the priestly and religious vocations or when you experience more austerities, difficulties, and privations, in your calling, rejoice and be glad. For it is at precisely these moments that your vocation and mission can be seen more clearly as more noble and worthy. Never is the image of God in you more clearly revealed. Have confidence, because it is when you are hung on the cross with the Lord that you will draw all things up there to him.

385. Do not think that your consecrated life has lost its meaning because you are unable to continue living in community or are prevented from performing works of charity, education, or assistance to those in need. What did Jesus do on the cross? What does he do in the tabernacle? He is present, praying, offering himself in sacrifice. How could you fail to see the meaning here? It was at the very moment of "uselessness" on the cross that the Lord redeemed mankind.

386. Even if you are not allowed to have schools and churches, even if you are denied access to radio, television, and other means of mass communication, do not complain that you lack the means to bring Jesus to the world. Rest assured, when God permits you to be deprived of everything, it means that nothing is indispensable to his work. When all else is denied you, follow the example of Mary in making God present in quieter, humbler ways. Remember Mary our mother!

387. The Church instructs us to celebrate the ceremony of religious profession during the Mass in order to remind the new religious that he offers God his life in union with the sacrifice of the altar. Therefore, during every Mass, renew your vows with all your heart and with all the meaning of a "new and everlasting covenant."

388. All the churches on the face of the earth could be destroyed, but wherever there is still one priest, we can still have the Mass, we can still have the Holy Eucharist.

Sixteen: Obedience

Joyful acceptance is a sign of holiness.

389. Did you vow obedience to your superiors or did your superiors vow to obey you?

390. The person of weak character who loses control of his will is like a mahout who cannot control an elephant. The obedient person who has mastered his will is like a circus trainer who controls tigers.

391. A disciplined army is a strong army. An obedient apostle is a strong and brave apostle.

392. You can accurately estimate how holy a person is by how readily and joyfully he obeys.

393. While the world may call such obedience folly, God nevertheless asks you to obey out of love of him. This obedience is heroic virtue, not folly.

394. Lucifer rebelled and still persists in inciting rebellion in the Church with his motto: "I will not serve."

395. Our divine Savior also led a revolution, which has been followed by millions upon millions. However, his motto was "Obedient unto death" (see Philippians 2:8).

396. Obedience allows for initiative, the search for understanding, and the presentation of different points of view. However, it also calls for careful listening, accepting instructions, and attentive implementation.

397. When it comes to submission, there are different categories of people: Some carry out instructions without resigning their own judgment, other submit and carry out orders because the superior is agreeable to them, and finally there are those who obey without reservation, completely for the love of God.

398. If your superior tells you to perform a difficult task, carry it out to the best of your ability and have trust. Is there any task as difficult as conquering the world empty-handed as the Lord sent his disciples out to do? The apostles obeyed and succeeded. Consider this ongoing miracle and have confidence.

399. You cannot expect your superior necessarily always to be

exemplary any more than you can reasonably expect your doctor always to be healthy. Exemplary conduct commands your respect, but to obey only because such conduct inspires you is to follow your own feelings rather than to practice the virtue of obedience.

400. If you do not act out of obedience, your work will not be pleasing to God, even if you succeed in carrying out some colossal tasks. God values your heart. He has no need of your works; he created the whole universe without your help.

401. As it is in the middle of human society while in this world, the Church needs a framework of human organization. One act of disobedience inflicts a wound of the common life of the Church just as much as one dysfunctional cell or vessel causes pain or discomfort in the whole human body.

402. Purity means dying to the flesh, obedience means dying to the will.

403. To carry out instructions while still struggling against them is pride, not obedience.

404. Learn not to be too trusting of yourself. Learn to discuss things with experienced people. Learn to have confidence that the hand of God arranges all things through many different people and circumstances.

405. Obey in silence: The truth will set you free. Silence for five years, ten years, your whole life. Silence in death. God knows

you and that is sufficient for now. On the last day, the whole of mankind will know.

406. Obedience is more important than sacrifice. Sacrifices can be of merely material things—fruits, incense, animals, money, etc. When you obey, however, you sacrifice yourself, you kill your own will and pride, to become a living holocaust.

Seventeen: Poverty

If the Lord is your inheritance,
why are you still not satisfied?

407. Your possessions will bury you if you wear them on your head or close to your heart. They will be your footstool if you stand on them.

408. "Be poor in the place you live, be poor in the clothes you wear, be poor in the food you eat, be poor in the things you use, be poor in the work you do" (Pere Chevrier).

409. The person who asks for little is always content because he considers himself to have sufficient. The person who demands much is extremely miserable because he keeps feeling deprived.

410. Looking at yourself, you feel deprived, you feel that you are the most miserable person in the world. Take a look

around you and see how many people are really worse off than you are.

411. To have no possessions while still yearning for them is not poverty. Having possessions, but being detached from them, is a sign of poverty in spirit.

412. Do not be generous with other people's possessions. Do not be stingy with your own possessions. Do not squander those things which properly belong to the entire community.

413. To be poor and humble, to be the lowest in society, to be poor materially, to be poor and suffering from insufficient food and shelter despite long and hard work—these are some instances of poverty. But poverty of spirit means accepting whatever circumstances of life you find yourself in.

414. Use riches with generosity, appreciate them with discernment, and be strongly detached from them, because they do not belong to you. God has merely entrusted them to you to share with the poor.

415. To quietly yield up your comfortable place or your profitable work is a sign of a genuine practice of poverty.

416. You are the Lord's steward, responsible for the possessions he has entrusted to you. If he entrusts you with many things, you have much to look after. If he entrusts you with little, you have little to look after. If he takes them back, you are content.

417. Poverty which is envious, poverty which is critical of others, and poverty which harbors resentment are three kinds of poverty which have nothing to do with the poverty of the gospel.

418. The world may not know you are obedient and may not understand your chastity, but it can easily recognize whether or not you are a witness to poverty.

419. "O Lord, let me be poor like you." How often do we make the opposite petition!

420. The expression "the Church of the poor" does not mean that we would have people stay poor, but rather that we endeavor to raise everyone up in every respect.

421. To possess as if not possessing; to sell as if not selling; to buy as if not buying; to act as if one has nothing at all; to be master of everything while demanding nothing, but rather to be prepared to give everything—this is the spirit of poverty.

422. Poverty does not mean deprivation of material possessions, which is better defined as destitution and wretchedness. Rather, poverty means the right understanding of material possessions. For example, do not say, "It's just a cup of coffee or a glass of beer." Your enjoyment of these might be the result of much toil, hardship, and even sacrifice on the part of those who produced them.

423. What is the most important aspect of poverty? It is work! This will be the consolation you feel when you understand

the significance of the fatigue of daily work: "Blessed is that servant whom his master when he comes will find so doing" (Luke 12:43).

424. When, as a young girl of fifteen, Clare sought to follow St. Francis, he asked her, "What is it that you seek in coming here?" Her response was clear and concise: "I am looking for God." She became a saint because God himself was her treasure. How many today know how to choose as she did?

Eighteen: Chastity

Shield the chaste heart with the
armor of prayer and sacrifice.

425. "Blessed are the pure in heart for they shall see God" (Matthew 5:8). Priests and religious are not the only people called to observe chastity. Rather, everyone must do so according to his or her state of life. The life of chastity is not a life of restriction, but a life of greater freedom.

426. There are many people who, while appearing to be angels of charity, are in fact devils of covetousness. Unhappy the community that meets with such an angel!

427. God grants the gift of chastity only to humble souls. Pray for it every day then with a simple and sincere heart, one that acknowledges its own weaknesses.

428. The proud will fall sooner or later; because they rely on their own strength rather than on God, he will allow them to stand alone on this shallow foundation.

429. The press is constantly calling for the protection of human and civil rights or joining in the struggle for them. Yet at the same time, the mass media themselves abuse their power by treating human beings as animals, exciting our animal instincts and poisoning our minds. Where are the people who are struggling? Where are the human rights agencies to protect us from these things?

430. You can drive the devil away and keep the world at a distance, but the flesh you will have to bear with you until the day you die.

431. If you want to be chaste, you must discipline yourself through sacrifice. Lilies are as white as alabaster and cherry blossoms are fragrantly beautiful because they have taken root deep in the heart of the earth, because they have held out against the attacks of storm and tempest, because they have endured the hands which prune them.

432. Without charity, chastity is meaningless. Otherwise, why do you safeguard your chastity? Is it because you are selfish and cannot tolerate anyone else? Or perhaps because no one could possibly love you? Or is it because you desire to devote your heart entirely to a greater love of God and neighbor? Only the last reason is a right motive.

433. There are many laypeople living exemplary lives of chastity in the midst of the world. On observing this, your consecrated soul should be awestruck with admiration and their example should spur you to make even greater efforts in your life.

434. Many young people today scoff at the idea of chastity, regarding it as old-fashioned when applied as a standard to them. But when they marry, they demand chastity from their spouses. Any unfaithfulness in their spouse is met with jealousy and even threats of suicide.

435. I have met many people from all walks of life and living in many different countries who have one thing in common: They live happy single lives in the world. Their secret? They all live a life of prayer.

436. Priests and religious will produce many reasons to rationalize their departure from the celibate state, but in the majority of cases the truth of the matter is that they are compelled to leave because they began some emotional involvement long after giving up prayer.

437. Mary Magdalene rose up and became a saint. When are you going to make your decision?

438. Do not claim that "The water failed to put out the fire." This is only because the fire is great and you have neglected to use enough water.

439. The flesh is the enemy's guerrilla, lying in wait for you. Books, newspapers, movies, and bad companions are its weapons, which day by day become more and more sophisticated. If you do not strengthen your defenses, namely, prayer, sacrifice, and recourse to the sacraments; if you do not wake up and keep watch; if you do not quell every slightest sign of rebellion; if you pamper the enemy guerrilla while casting aside your allies, the saints and good companions—then do not be surprised when you are violently attacked and conquered.

440. Excessive eating and drinking is the open door for the demon of impurity.

441. How can a doctor cure a patient who insists that he is not sick, refuses to be examined, and will not take any medication?

442. Without chastity, your apostolate is a fraud.

443. Do not say, "I love them because they love me." You have to love yourself first. What would you accept in exchange for your soul?

444. Do not make peace with lust any more than you would make peace with a disease. In both cases, it is a matter of life and death.

445. Your heart is not made of stone. It is precious because it is made of flesh and is capable of love. Take hold of the cross courageously, with both hands, and place it in your heart.

446. Telling obscene stories, even for the sake of amusement, is not profitable. Never tell such stories. Experience shows that those who tell such stories will sooner or later act them out. That is what psychological warfare is all about.

447. Do not engage in conversation with the demon of impurity, just as you would not stand by and watch the testing of an atomic weapon. Flight is the best strategy.

448. The saints were as weak as you are, some were even weaker. They differed only in their great determination, through which they gained merit and became saints.

449. The flesh is always very fragile. No matter what or how much covering you put on, the flesh will always be there beneath the layers.

450. The value of your body is that . . .
    . . . it was redeemed by the blood of the Lord Jesus;
    . . . it is the temple of the Holy Trinity;
    . . . it is meant to be glorious for all eternity.
    Therefore, do not put it up for sale!

451. The attractions offered by the agents of the demon of impurity are very alluring and the defending barrier of the flesh pleads strongly. Do not enter into dialogue with them. After a short moment of pleasure, you will have nothing but boredom, loneliness, and remorse. Why exchange heaven for hell?

452. The demon of impurity fears two things: fasting and prayer. Have you been practicing these?

453. The worst happens when you become self-satisfied, reject the warnings of others, and begin to present yourself with a "Certificate of Grade A Chaste Conduct."

454. Never despise a neighbor who may have fallen while you have stood firm. If you have stood firm until now, it is only due to the grace of God. Take care, lest tomorrow you should fall even more than your neighbor!

455. To relax your guard over your senses is to open the gates of the fortress before the enemy's onslaught.

456. Every time you get up again, take hold of your weapons and fight with all your might. Remember, the demon of impurity has a very subtle "disarmament" policy.

457. One defeat does not lose the war. God can bring good out of anything, even sin.

458. I neither wish to know nor want to remember the past of my neighbors. I simply think about them in the present in order that we may love and support one another and in the future that we may foster confidence and encourage one another.

459. If you truly strive to live a life of chastity, you will find your

will-power strengthened, because it is trained only amid valiant struggle.

460. I have even greater confidence in the Lord when I see how he defended and forgave sinners: "Let him who is without sin among you be the first to throw a stone at her. . . . Neither do I condemn you; go, and do not sin again" (John 8:7, 11).

461. People cannot understand chastity: Some think it is mad; some think it is difficult; some think it has no value. Nevertheless, in God's eyes, it has great value. A true life of chastity can be realized only with the help of God, who alone can give meaning to chastity.

Nineteen: The Family

The family is the Church in microcosm.

462. Human happiness is not based on possessions or position, but on the love experienced throughout the course of life.

463. To prepare priests, we have the seminary. To prepare religious, we have the novitiate. To prepare teachers, we have colleges of education. But what do have to prepare parents? Nothing at all! This is an enormous omission in our world. The church may offer some marriage preparation classes, but these have yet to have a great effect. How many people will be the victims of the adventure on which we seem to throw them so unprepared?

464. Reflect for a moment on the wedding feast at Cana. Initially, the guests were concerned with feasting and making

merry until they found that the wine had run out and all they had left was water. They then made a request to Jesus, in response to which he changed the water into a wine better than the one they had been drinking.

Remember that your own strength and resources are limited, and that while it is often not easy to persevere in love, God's grace is available to assist you, to intensify your love, and to secure happiness for your family. Therefore, do not forget to make room for the treasure of religion among your family heirlooms.

465. When you are young, you can go wherever you wish. When you grow older, perhaps someone else will hold your hand—and perhaps many little hands as well—will grasp you and take you where you might not want to go, where you believed you would never have the strength to go. Remember, love is able to assist you to do everything!

466. Married couples, both in their mutual love for each other and in their love for their children, fully live out Christ's love for all humankind. Through this love, they participate in and live again the mystery of redemption. Loving couples exercise this love to the full and without limits, in the same way the Lord loves them and loves everybody.

467. Marital love has the power to stir up in the human heart all courage, confidence, and generosity.

468. To look for a change in one's partner without helping by

love to effect that change only brings frustration to one's life companion. But to expect no change brought about by love is to underestimate him or her.

469. The love given to help your spouse grow is the means for that growth. To force your spouse to change as a prerequisite for love is to eliminate completely all means to that growth.

470. The sure way to secure a change in your life's companion is to accept him or her as you first did—in love.

Change occurs only when one knows and feels one is loved.

471. Love is always full of expectation, not because you are doubtful of your spouse's love, but because you feel you have the responsibility to create for each other things which are new, stimulating, and different, realities of which you were previously unaware. This expectation is itself a source of happiness for you.

472. There is an unfortunate human propensity to judge everyone on the basis of their past. But there is also the perception, born of love, which foresees how much people can change for the better.

473. Love is not blind. True love sees the weaknesses of the beloved and tries to shoulder these burdens. It also sees the strengths and subtly tries to encourage their potential.

474. If a person cannot love the flesh of his flesh and bone of his bones, or if he cannot bring happiness to this fundamental unit

which is the basis of all human society, how can such a person even think of trying to reform the world?

475. In our time the Church has mapped out a spirituality of marriage which allows us to see that marriage is the means by which the human race is to develop and flourish and that it is thus truly a vocation to holiness.

476. Are you surprised to hear talk of "the vocation to be parents of a family?" People make a great mistake when they restrict the concept of vocation—that is, a calling to a state of perfection—to priests and religious. After all, when two people, by means of the sacrament of marriage, solemnly promise to love one another in Christ for their lives, is this not a statement of faith, a profession of vows?

477. If the laity are to define their particular mission in the world, then they should find that their most important and definite mission is the life of the family.

478. Reform the family in order to reform the Church.

479. Give up that mistaken view which thinks of laypeople as solitary, unattached individuals who belong to no community. Also get rid of that simplistic and negative habit of categorizing the laity as simply those who are not priests or religious.

Do not forget that the majority of laypeople live in families which understand and live the sacrament of marriage.

480. It is such a pity that the only things the modern world knows of the Catholic doctrine concerning marriage are some of its prohibitions. From these, the world derives not even an inkling that Christ came to redeem man's love and that through the sacrament of matrimony he enriched the status of humankind in an extraordinary way. Therefore, it is your duty to study the many beautiful, positive aspects of Christian marriage.

481. We have to strive, in both the doctrinal and the pastoral aspects of marriage, to convince Christian families of their own strength. They must discover that they are not merely passive recipients of the teachings and sacraments of the Church and the grace of God, but that there is also an active component to their marriage which calls them to be apostolic.

482. Aware of their unique mission, many Catholic families place the human and supernatural forces of their conjugal love and sacrament of matrimony under the authority and at the disposal of the Church, often doing this with remarkable devotion.

483. To love your spouse is to act in accord with the will of God. When you realize this, you will understand that you can fulfill your vocation in the ordinary circumstances of your life by making every trifling activity a response to the call of God. This knowledge should revolutionize your whole life.

484. The love between husband and wife is an image, a sign of

the love of Christ for the Church. In this mystery you will discover dignity, strength, and unity.

The love between husband and wife is an extension of the love of God. How uplifting and encouraging for the married couple is this love!

485. God has given you a loving spouse and beautiful children so that you may help one another to become holy. What have you done with this?

486. Remember . . . that you and your spouse are responsible for mutual growth to maturity in the love of God;

. . . that your vocation is to be together and to reach sanctity through this dependence on each other;

. . . that in this task there is available to you an unceasing supply of grace from the sacrament of matrimony;

. . . that you are encouraged to live fervently the mystery of the Lord's death and resurrection in every aspect of your lives.

487. You must discover that you can—and indeed, have the duty to—sanctify yourselves in and through marriage.

488. All the events in your lives as husband and wife and parents, and all your social responsibilities, are opportunities for you to grow, to deny yourselves, and to advance along the path of true holiness.

489. The unity between husband and wife must be absolutely complete: a unity of body, mind, love, and spirit, through the

presence of Christ. To love each other in God is very beautiful, to love each other for God's sake even more so. Your whole family must listen to God attentively and then advance together in intimacy with him.

490. Quiet moments spent side by side with each other immersed in thought, moments spent praying spontaneously for one another and your children, moments spent exchanging intimacies concerning your spiritual life and your apostolate—to the Christian couple, these moments are moments of revelation and profound, heartfelt joy.

491. Bringing children into the world is not only a response to the need to carry on family lineage, but it is also a response to the desire to increase the Mystical Body. The education of children is the training of those who will continue the faithful worship of God our Father. Discover and admire this noble design which God has for our families.

492. Your duty as parents requires that you guide your children along the way in every respect and to every virtue. And when you train them to be active members of the Mystical Body of Christ, you are showing them how to be children of God.

493. The family is a microcosm of the Church, it is truly *Ecclesiuncula*, the Church in miniature. Thus, in a mystical way, the Lord is present in his life, death, and resurrection in the lives of each member of the family. This reflection enlightens the meaning and changes the life of the Christian family.

494. The truth of the family as a microcosm of the Church should help us to see more clearly the primacy and mission of the family in the following ways:

1) The family perpetuates the Church which Jesus Christ established in the world.
2) The presence of God is realized in the head of the family.
3) It is the role of the father to perform the duty of priest in the family.
4) The family witnesses to the presence of the Church in its day-to-day life.
5) The efforts of the family to raise itself up to God also serve to help the entire Church to advance.
6) The family strengthens the communion between God and each one of its individual members.

495. Christ desired to build up his Mystical Body by means of family units. The Church is free to alter its methods of preaching and can change its methods of organization, but it must always expand by means of its families. The faith is transmitted through these dynamic family units.

496. The education of children can be a "school of perfection" for parents. Children possess a critical outlook and are keen observers. They will oblige you to fulfill your role sincerely, thereby helping you yourself to advance.

497. You can be assured that the life of a truly Christian family is a very special way of life.

498. If we maintain that the world of work must be sanctified by workers, we must likewise insist that the Christian family is the first apostle to other families.

499. The world evaluates Christian marriage by the standard of holiness in Christian families.

500. Morning and night prayers in the family—or, to put it more accurately, times of family prayer—fulfill the obligation to form a community of Christians, a unity of the Church, according to the words of Jesus: "For where two or three are gathered in my name, there am I in the midst of them" (Matthew 18:20).

501. The Christian family must be apostolic in its witness. It must show that it has been called to holiness and that it can live a married life pleasing to God. It must share with other families the grace and happiness with which God has blessed it.

502. The family is meant to be a fount of light shining in the darkness of our world. If only more families were like this, the world would become one big, happy family, filled with light and hope.

503. The Christian family can be apostolic through its hospitality. Open wide your hearts when you open wide your homes. Hospitality is the most convenient and natural way to witness to your love, unity, joy, happiness, and openness to others. The art of hospitality can thus become the apostolate of hospitality. Live in such a way that anyone who visits you will be encouraged by your example to want to live like you.

504. When you sit side by side together in the presence of God, it is a time of truth, a wonderful unfolding, a dose of immortal medicine. It is in this way that the atmosphere of the family will be changed and problems will be solved in a spirit of mutual understanding. Whereas before this husband and wife have lived together in a sort of peaceful coexistence, they are now one in love, one in happiness, one in difficulties, and one in prayer.

505. The first seminary, the first novitiate, the first college, is the Christian family. No teacher, no matter how talented or gifted, can replace parents. If this fundamental unit breaks down, the future of the Church and of human society will become shakier and shakier, until they both finally collapse.

Pope John XXIII recognized this principle in simple, but beautiful, words worth recalling. On the day he reached fifty years of age, he wrote to his parents: "Dear Mama and Papa, today I have reached fifty. God has given me many positions in the Church, I have been to many places, I have studied much . . . but no schooling has given me more instruction or has been more beneficial than that which I received when I sat on your laps."

Twenty: Humility

Learn from the Lord how to be meek and humble.

506. If you understand the happiness which comes from being a child of God, humiliations will take nothing away from you and acclaim will add nothing to you.

507. If you really knew yourself, you would find it amusing that some people praise you and logical that others hold you in contempt. In fact, you would be surprised that they do not treat you even more harshly.

508. An apostle is humble and gives the credit to God for everything.

509. When you downgrade yourself, you are not necessarily practicing humility. When others downgrade you, you are not

necessarily practicing humility, either. When others downgrade you and you accept it out of love for God, however, then you are truly being humble.

510. Only by contemplating the entire life of Jesus Christ will you be able truly to understand humility. For love of us, the Son of God demeaned himself for thirty-three years to the point of accepting from the people of his day every imaginable foolishness, ignorance, malice, and rejection.

511. In your pride, you plunder God's grace and glory, foolishly trying to make them your property, your merit.

512. Follow the example of our mother, Mary. The more humble she was, the more glorious she became because through her humility, she was able to see the marvelous things which God had brought about in her soul. Humility is to the soul what glass is to a lightbulb: The clearer the glass, the more light passes without hindrance.

513. The person who lives in the presence of God cannot be proud since he realizes that he has nothing to be proud about. Everything, after all, belongs to God.

514. Do not feign humility when you refuse something. Humility is not a pretext for avoiding your duty to commit yourself to God, even if the commitment runs the risk of failure and disgrace in the eyes of the world.

515. Do not deny or repress your talents and abilities. Just remember to thank God for having chosen to use these gifts of yours as tools in his great work, just as an artist may use a cheap brush to execute a masterpiece.

516. Only those who are humble will find true peace and happiness from the Lord who invites us to "Take my yoke upon you, and learn from me; for I am gentle and lowly in heart, and you will find rest for your souls. For my yoke is easy and my burden is light" (Matthew 11:29–30).

517. The humble person is like the man who stoops so low, close to the ground, that he cannot fall any further. The proud person is like the one who climbs to the top of a high tower, from where it is all that much easier to have a terrible fall.

518. Determination to obey the Church is loyalty; to take drastic measures for the sake of duty is courage, not pride.

519. As long as you go on worshipping your own ego, you are not unlike the person whose "prayer" consists of the litany, "O Lord, believe in me. O Lord, hope in me."

520. The most bitter trial is having to come to an acceptance of your own limitations. It is like being nailed to a cross. If the cross is broad, the suffering is mitigated somewhat by the leeway this gives you. But if the cross is narrow, the agony is that much the greater.

521. During his earthly ministry, Jesus had a special love for the humble which overlooked their sins and forgave them, never mentioning their sins again—look at the cases of Peter, Mary Magdalene, and Zacchaeus, to name just a few. The Lord entered their homes, despite the knowledge that his kindness would earn him a reputation as a "friend of tax collectors and sinners" (Luke 7:34).

522. While it is not always possible to avoid tension, it is possible to diminish it. First, remember that God does not demand that you do everything. Second, as to those things he has entrusted to you, he will always give you the means and the strength to carry them out. If, with all your efforts and good will, you cannot fulfill these tasks, then it is God's will that it should not be you to bring them to completion. Do not be tense and disappointed. Be serene in his hands!

Twenty-One: Restraint of Speech

*Restraining your tongue is like
burying a seed deep in the earth.*

523. Jesus Christ was the Word made Flesh, but in order to fulfill his mission in obedience to the Father, he was silent for thirty of his thirty-three years on earth before preaching a single word and then was silent again during his passion.

524. The more circumspect you are, the fewer regrets you will have.

525. Do not expect other people to become convinced of your opinion just because you talk a lot. In fact, the more you talk, the more you will expose the flaws in your position. Worse still, as you continue talking, everyone will begin to see this, and you will then be progressively obliged to redefine and correct each of your successive utterances.

526. When the Lord performed miracles, he forbade publicity about them. He even forbade his disciples to speak of his Transfiguration on Mount Tabor. You should follow this example. Pray and meditate about your apostolic ideas and then carry them out to the best of your ability with the assistance of the Holy Spirit, disregarding the world and what it may think about what you are doing.

527. In the Scriptures, we have some wonderful examples of what heroic deeds can be performed when one is circumspect: including Judith in the Old Testament and the Virgin Mary in the New Testament. On the other hand, we also have examples of what can result from lack of circumspection, such as the conquest of Samson by Delilah.

528. The seed which falls and is hidden away deep in the earth will yield rich fruits and flowers, but the seed which falls on the highways will either be snatched up by birds or be crushed under by passing traffic and be wasted.

529. Every time you are tempted to boast about your abilities, every time you are provoked to quarrel, every time you feel anger: Be silent. In these times, no matter how wise or right you may be, be silent. Otherwise, you will end up doing more damage than you intended.

530. So many of your writings, so many of your speeches, and so many of your important plans and projects have originated from the deep recesses of your mind and heart. For it is in the

hidden, silent depths of your being that you find the fundamentals: sacrifice, patience, reflection, and love.

531. Circumspection is not secretive. Rather, it is common sense and prudence. For example, you would not want other people to expose your private life to public discussion and debate. But when you go about constantly reminding people to keep secrets you have divulged, have you not just betrayed all secrets and proven that you are unable to keep confidences?

Twenty-Two: Joy

Offer each other the gift of happiness.

532. Holiness entails neither long faces nor being sad and miserable. Holiness consists rather in being continuously happy because it is the possession of God.

533. Do not be downcast. If only you would have a supernatural outlook, you would see everything in a new light.

534. Why are you unhappy? Is it because something is disturbing your relationship with God? In that case, examine yourself to see at once what it is.

535. You should always be happy. The Road of Hope is a joyful road which admits no sadness.

536. If you are doing God's work, how is it that you feel discouraged? The more difficult things become, the happier you should be, just as Peter and John were after they had been flogged: "They left the presence of the council, rejoicing that they were counted worthy to suffer dishonor for the name" (Acts 5:41).

537. When you are successful, give thanks to God. When you fail, likewise give thanks to God, for it is when you fail that he tests your commitment to his work. In fact, to be joyful and courageous during times of failure is much more difficult than being joyful in times of good fortune: You can count the number of heroes of the first kind with the fingers of one hand.

538. If you are always morose, pessimistic, and critical, people will begin to doubt that eloquent advice which you constantly dish out. After all, seeing your example, will they still keep their faith in the God you preached?

539. Be happy
    . . . with those who love you;
    . . . with those who hate you;
    . . . when all is joyful and bright for you;
    . . . when your heart suffers deeply;
    . . . when everyone follows you;
    . . . when you are alone and abandoned.
    Be happy always and lead everyone you meet to experience this same joy, even if you may often feel brokenhearted. To act in this way requires a greater holiness than all the fasting and acts of self-denial you can perform put together.

540. You have no money? You have no gift to give? You have nothing at all? Are you forgetting that you have the gift of happiness to present to others, the gift of a peace which the world cannot give, a treasure of joy which knows no bounds.

541. How do you rid yourself of sadness? Pray! And why pray? Because it is through prayer that you come to meet the Lord, just as Mary Magdalene did while searching for his body or as did the two disciples on the road to Emmaus. In the joy of this meeting, all three of them quickly forgot their grief and distress.

542. "Rejoice, in so far as you share Christ's sufferings, that you may also rejoice and be glad when his glory is revealed" (1 Peter 4:13).

Twenty-Three: Wisdom

The cross is the book that teaches true wisdom.

543. "The word of the cross is folly to those who are perishing, but to us who are being saved it is the power of God" (1 Corinthians 1:18).

544. When you are being praised or denigrated, neither be saddened, on the one hand, because you fear you are losing something, nor be joyful, on the other, because you think you are gaining something: neither is the case. There is only one thing which can harm you, sin, and only one thing which can increase your worth, virtue. You should not concern yourself with either praise or criticism, any more than you would be afraid of a toy gun or eager to possess counterfeit money.

545. Who will "scatter the proud in the imagination of their hearts" and "put down the mighty from their thrones" (Luke

1:51–52)? Who will restore order to a world of confused and erroneous thinking? Who will bring peace to the people of our time so that they will be able to travel the Road of Hope freely? There is only one answer: the Wisdom whom God bestowed on us through our mother Mary, the Seat of Wisdom.

546. The world of the poor writhes in hunger and thirst, it is dragged in all directions except forward by all-too-many social problems which defy solution. Poverty enchains wisdom!

In contrast, the world of capitalist materialism wallows in a sea of pleasure. Creating extra "needs" in society, it increasingly confuses the mind with disquiet and discord. In its propaganda it elevates itself to the place of teacher of the world. But such pride causes the loss of wisdom.

547. The world is changed not by action, but by ideas which direct action.

548. When scholars and scientists—who today often think they know everything and have discovered everything—kneel down in prayer before God and humbly acknowledge that their discoveries are made only through grace from above, they will come to see the universe through different eyes. They will see that everything has been arranged in accord with a perfect order and a perfect plan from all eternity.

549. Scientific geniuses have contributed much to the advancement of civilization. Yet they possess only a small portion of the

light and truth. A world which possesses such splendid order as ours does requires, however, an overriding supreme wisdom. This wisdom is the Word and "through him all things were made" (The Nicene Creed).

550. "The Word became flesh" (John 1:14) and God the Father proclaimed, "This is my beloved Son, with whom I am well pleased; listen to him" (Matthew 17:5). Thus we know that:

- He is the Way: follow in his footsteps.
- He is the Truth: believe only the word that he teaches.
- He is the Life: live only by his spirit.

551. Do not lose confidence when you see that the Road of Hope eludes some people whom the world regards as wise. Our Lord forewarned us of this: "I thank thee, Father, Lord of heaven and earth, that thou hast hidden these things from the wise and understanding and revealed them to babes" (Matthew 11:25). Thank God for bestowing on you his true wisdom.

552. The world is afraid of this wisdom because it upsets the old life, rebukes the world, and overturns set values—in short, human nature finds it hard to accept. Nevertheless, humble souls of good will and those little ones fired with youthful enthusiasm have, throughout every period of history, followed this wisdom successfully to the end.

553. The wisdom which the Holy Spirit bestows will illumine

your thoughts, guide your plans, and transform your actions by giving them an eternal value. It will transform you into an immortal child of the Spirit.

554. Have confidence and follow the example of St. Paul: "When I came to you, brethren, I did not come proclaiming to you the testimony of God in lofty words or wisdom. For I decided to know nothing among you except Jesus Christ and him crucified" (1 Corinthians 2:1–2).

555. The crucifixion of the Lord is the wisdom that comes from heaven. As the experience of the past twenty centuries has clearly shown, it accomplished a brilliant revolution that could neither be concealed nor held back. Consequently, many courageous souls have volunteered and continue to do so in the service of this wisdom.

556. If you desire wisdom, pray earnestly for it, entrusting your whole life to God without reservation. Then, should a crisis occur (even if you are dragged before a court) it will no longer be you who speak, but the Holy Spirit speaking through you. Remember the example of Stephen who preached when filled with the Holy Spirit (see Acts 6:9–10).

Twenty-Four: Studies

To study is to pray.

557. If you want to make rapid and substantial progress and advance along the Road of Hope: Study.

558. The time of study is a time of prayer.

559. "You shall love the Lord your God with all your heart, and with all your soul, and with all your strength, and with all your mind" (Luke 10:27). If you do not study so as to develop your full potential, you will not be able to serve others as completely as you should: Thus, you will not be loving God as fully as you should.

560. Study to learn, to reform, to serve, and to love.

561. Whoever has ten coins has to earn ten more; whoever has five must earn five more; and whoever has one must earn one

more (see Luke 19:13–25). The moral is when you are in a position to learn, your responsibility to study is all the more serious.

562. The obligation to study does not necessarily require joining a class or taking up literature or science. However, it does mean a general obligation to exercise and improve your abilities, to perfect your work, and to strive to keep pace with an ever-changing world.

563. If you desire a world revolution, God's grace is needed. You yourself, however, must first become a competent instrument for it.

564. Would you knowingly place yourself in the hands of an inexperienced doctor or pilot? Probably not. But there can be equally disastrous consequences whenever any person with other responsibilities is incompetent.

565. Look upon your occupation as a vocation to carry out God's will in society and you will sanctify your work.

566. Sacrifices for your work, diligence in cultural matters, service to the cause of science—all of these are highly commendable. Only remember that they are the means, not the end.

567. Put your knowledge into practice! Theory and knowledge are not mutually exclusive. Practice leads you closer to reality where you will discover that things are often more easily said than done. The lesson you should learn from this simple

observation is to be less critical of other people while increasing your self-examination.

568. The Church needs intelligent minds to carry the love of God to all corners of the world. But it also suffers from the division and confusion often caused by these minds, which can be arrogant and conceited in addition to being intelligent. The fallen angels were such a case.

569. Laziness is the root of all evil and is thus shunned by the apostle. There are no retired apostles, only apostles who may change their means of working to suit their changing strength and ability.

570. When you are young, your life is filled with hope, you fervently practice virtue and improve your talents. Make sure that this sense of bright optimism permeates all your efforts with an apostolic idealism.

571. If you go up in an airplane and look down, you will look upon the traffic, houses, people, and various objects and see them as if they were little toys. If you were to go up into space, you would see how small the earth is. Thus the more you study, the more you increase your knowledge, the more humble you should become and the more you should desire to learn.

572. The Church exists in the midst of the world. The whole of knowledge and science can be used to defend and promote the truths of the Church in the world. Thus, the more you apply yourself to study, the more you will be of service to the Church.

573. The more knowledgeable a person becomes, the more he will realize his limitations. Only ignorant people think their knowledge is unlimited.

574. Many so-called Christian intellectuals conceal in their academic or social lives the Christian side of their characters. They think they can put on or take off their Christianity like a shirt whenever it suits them.

575. Think of all the progress you would have made by now if you had memorized just one new thought every day or if you had read just one extra book every month. If you have not done so up to now, begin at once. Today.

576. If you are not an expert, it is easy for you to be pretentious and make foolhardy statements. And if you happen to be in a high position, it is all the easier for you to create the illusion of your alleged expertise. Your incompetence in these circumstances would be all the more deplorable since your posturing could bring disaster upon yourself and many others.

577. It is not enough to be talented: One must also be virtuous. Talented people who are also proud and difficult can only use their talents to deal with material things: They lack the sensitivity required to deal with human relationships.

578. To consider yourself a specialist in every field is an idea which is fast becoming out of date. Today if you wish to serve,

you must be able to enlist the cooperation of others in every field of knowledge.

579. A diploma will attest only to the fact that you possessed a particular level of knowledge and expertise at the time of a particular examination. If your study ends there, even a pile of diplomas will not guarantee your continued standing as an expert.

580. You ask: "How long will I have to study?" My answer: unceasingly. The world is changing, the work of and demands on the Church are ever new and fresh. The instruments of the Church must therefore be continually sharpened. God does not bestow the wisdom of Solomon or the understanding and insight of Mary on lazy people.

581. The more you seek to understand a truth, the more you will understand it. And the more you devote yourself to the defense of Truth, the more thoroughly you will know it.

Twenty-Five: Development

Humankind has the honor and obligation
of conquering and liberating.

582. In reality, development is not concerned solely with the feeding and clothing of people, or the improvement of agricultural methods, or the digging of wells and canals. Rather, true development means the promotion of human dignity in all respects so that people may live in a manner worthy of beings "created in the image of God" (Genesis 1:27).

583. Do not be content just because you may have helped someone. Do not think that it is sufficient just to give alms to those in need. No, God requires something more from you: He wants you to help those less fortunate in such a way that they will be able to help themselves now and any others who may come after them.

584. God desires our collaboration in the work of creation, as well as that of redemption. If God were to work alone, the work would be more perfect, but his mankind would be less noble. Follow God's way.

585. Our Lord taught that whenever we complete a task, we should withdraw and admit our own incapacity. This teaching, often overlooked, is an intensely profound insight. Our incapacity stems from our being a mere instrument through which God's grace works. This incapacity renders our efforts to seek gratitude from others or to keep them dependent upon us thoroughly futile: They have already been set free.

586. I have four counsels for you:

1) Allow others to advance, yielding your position to them.
2) Give them less, but demand more from them.
3) Teach them how to help others.
4) Do not relish your position as a benefactor.

Rather, strive to be a neighbor to everyone and to serve all whom you encounter.

587. No matter how much better off others may be because of the assistance which you lent them, it cannot be said that you have brought about their true development if you have let them become robots.

588. The tragedy of poverty lies not in destitution, but in the fact

that the poor often cannot live in a way befitting human beings.

589. Foreman and laborer, officer and private soldier, teacher and student—each of these differs from the other in rank and position. These differences, however, are only superficial. People travel in company with each other because they are human, because they are children of God, and this is the only important thing. Remember: "No longer do I call you servants, for the servant does not know what his master is doing; but I have called you friends, for all that I heard from my Father I have made known to you" (John 15:15).

590. The best gift you can give to your servant is not a nice dress, or a good pair of shoes, or a new watch. It is the gift of your humanity, that brotherly love that is present throughout the day and shown in quiet, simple gestures woven into the routine of daily life.

591. The Lord could have chosen passive people to cooperate with him in his work, but he decided instead to accept sinners with all their impetuousness and complexities of character.

592. It is easy for you to help those easygoing people who only wish to follow or to be helped, those who are content to receive what you have to offer and to acknowledge you unconditionally as their leader. You should, however, seek to assist those responsible people who want to stand on their own feet, because it is their behavior that is more in accord with human dignity.

593. It may be hard, but you should motivate yourself to help others to stand up for themselves, to think for themselves, to organize among themselves, to fight for themselves, and, if need be, even to oppose your ideas. You will be much happier when you find them progressing along with you, rather than because of you.

594. Nuclear energy is an enormous breakthrough and justifiably the pride of our times. Few people today, however, seem to know how to harness this power for peace and development, and fewer still seem to know how to worship and praise the power of God which brought this potential about. On the other hand, all too many people today have seized control of this gift of the heavenly Father to manufacture weapons of destruction which daily become more frightening.

595. The human race offends God terribly by its abuse of his gifts, directing them to unjust purposes and fratricide.

596. It is not the world which has run out of living space, but rather the human heart which has become crowded out. It is not that all of the earth's agricultural products will be used up, but rather that human beings are at the point of devouring themselves with a ferocity beyond that of wild beasts.

597. If you would stop giving lectures about the drought in Ethiopia, the unrest in Bangladesh, or the violence in Latin America, for just long enough, you would notice that Jesus Christ, in the

person of your neighbor, is being abandoned and that his gospel is not being adequately preached in your own community, in the house next door, or even under your own roof.

598. People today take pride in all kinds of things: the power of the atom, the exploitation of natural resources, the increased power of missiles, the new spacecraft . . . indeed this is an era of seemingly boundless technological potential. However, if the human race abandons the purpose of development or forgets God whom the Creed professes to be "maker of heaven and earth, of all things visible and invisible," this pride will end by reducing the earth to dust and ashes.

599. Tragedy lies not so much in the hunger, thirst, and misery of poor countries, as in the indifference of the nations of the world to this enslavement and exploitation.

600. "Development is the new term for peace" (Pope Paul VI).

601. So long as developed countries fail to set aside so much as 1 percent of their incomes to help poorer countries to develop, so long as 20 percent of the world's population controls 80 percent of its resources, the danger of nuclear war cannot be avoided.

602. The planning and execution of one program of aid to true development which does not exploit the recipients will do more to restore peace than all the arms limitation conferences put together.

603. As Pope Paul VI urged repeatedly, you must become an apostle of development. Indeed, he will be remembered as the traveling evangelist of true peace and development.

604. In a manner of speaking, development could be defined as a world in which the "last will and testament" of Jesus Christ is being fulfilled: that all love, help, and share with one another in a spirit of universal brotherhood.

Twenty-Six: Dedication

*You should be willing to lay down
your life as Jesus did.*

605. Dedication does not consist of throwing yourself into a feverish round of activity. Dedication is much more profound. It means following the example of Jesus in loving others to the point of forgetting yourself completely for their sakes. It means offering yourself completely and without reservation in order to unite with others, to enrich them, and to help bring the work of God in their lives to a successful completion.

606. Humanity is truly "in the image of God" (Genesis 1:27) when people give of themselves continuously in imitation of the Persons of the Trinity, who are totally self-giving, totally related to each other, and totally absolute in their love.

607. You must become yourself, according to the will and with the grace of God, by releasing the divine image within you from the dust and camouflage which currently obscure it. You must be like the sculptor who chisels and files away at a piece of rock so that the features of the image already inside can be seen.

608. When you help others to forget themselves in order to dedicate themselves, you are really helping them to manifest the image of God already present in them.

609. The moment in which you offer yourself is in itself an exercise in learning how to sacrifice, because to speak of offering yourself is easy while the reality of the offering is difficult. Many people call for self-sacrifice, but few persevere in it.

610. During the course of the day, the occasions which present themselves for you to make an oblation of yourself are not really moments of suffering or loss; rather, they are a challenge from God for you to grow.

611. You must yourself be on the Road of Hope if you are to dedicate yourself or to call others to a life of dedication. On this road, the greatest service you can render to anyone is to help them to conform themselves to the image of God in Christ.

612. You ask me, "What is the measure of self-giving?" My reply is to remind you of the words of St. John: "By this we know love, that he laid down his life for us; and we ought to lay down our lives for the brethren" (1 John 3:16). Do what Jesus did and lay

down your life. If you have to make grand announcements of what you are doing; if your activities lack commitment; if you are careless in the practice of your faith; if you are afraid of starvation, poverty, imprisonment, or death; if you are willing only to dedicate yourself to "saving" those who are already saved . . . if any of these things apply to you, it would be better if you cease your involvement in the apostolate. Your dedication is counterfeit and has a commercial basis: You are concerned only with the dividends you hope to gain.

613. You should not do things for yourself alone, but for others as well. You should not only dedicate yourself but you should also strive to invite others to dedicate themselves. You should not look for sympathy for yourself, but rather you should urge others to widen the circles of their affection to enclose those around them, like a stone thrown into a pond which produces ever-widening circles of ripples. If you do these things, you will help to conform humanity to the plan God has decreed from all eternity.

614. Why are you feeling an incompleteness in your life, a loss of direction? Why do you feel restless? Is it not perhaps because you have yet to dispel that heavy dark cloud of sin which eclipses the image of God in your soul?

615. Many around us, in fact the whole of humanity, are struggling to find their way through a terrible mist. We must dedicate our lives to building a bridge of hope which will lead them to God, who is their supreme goal, everlasting love, and total

fulfillment. In him, no one is estranged from another, and we are all brothers and sisters.

616. Some people turn their faces away so as not to see, while others stop their ears so as not to hear. Nevertheless, truth remains truth despite them. See clearly, listen carefully. Reality is a lesson to be learned from your neighbor who is the teacher.

617. Sociologists and psychologists analyze reality by means of often-complicated statistical estimations according to their respective disciplines. Do not necessarily disregard their investigations, but rather gather up the questions they raise and examine them through the eyes of faith.

618. Look around you and you will see hundreds of thousands of young people neglected and living without a future. They dream endlessly of building a new world, a new humanity, but these dreams are being quashed by experience with drugs, violence, vice, lies, and discouragement. These young people need you, they appeal to you. Their appeal is the cry of a drowning swimmer, the entreaty of a suffocating man.

619. There are several varieties of dedication that you should be acquainted with:

There are those who, after a period of free and wholehearted dedication, are inclined to doubt the value of the struggle. They lose heart and retreat into the consolation of their private prayer saying, "I am afraid of forgetting God." They are wrong in their approach however: They should persevere in both prayer and active commitment.

There are others who throw themselves entirely, soul and body, into the struggle. But, in order to have their hands "free" for the fight, they dispense with God altogether. At first, their attitude is, "I will remember God after I have succeeded." However, this attitude gradually changes into one of, "This is the business of human beings, it's me who must make the effort. It has nothing to do with God, so leave him out of it."

Finally, there are those others still who will neither flee the battlefield nor betray the mission which God entrusted to them. They firmly believe in gaining a victory only with Christ. These are the only people who can truly say with all their hearts, "I dedicate myself to Christ."

620. Are you one of those pious Christians who, having spent all of their time in the shadow of a church, have become part angel, part saint, and remain only part human? Follow Jesus: true God and true man. Become fully human again.

621. Do not leave everyone else to build up the world while you yourself remain unaware and uninvolved, as if you did not even know what this means. The Lord has redeemed you. He has entrusted you with a mission, placing you in this world, in this time, in this place, for a reason. He placed you here as a human being, not some rock. There is a big difference! You have a purpose!

622. The most disastrous scandal of our time is the separation

between the practice of religion within church buildings and the practice of religion outside in society.

623. Although you may not be able to fathom its depths or probe its meaning, an effective revolution, capable of renewing the world, reaches from your heart to all the political, economic, and social structures of the world. This revolution, however, cannot be realized without both human beings and God. It is realized by humankind in Christ and with Christ. Dedicate yourself to this revolution.

624. For some time now, I have seen you come close to God, but you have not seen him, you have not met him. You do not lean on him or converse with him, hence you do not act with him. Thus, your soul is not at peace. Your problem? You try to confine God to a church building.

625. As a Christian, your dedication must differ from that of non-Christians since you see ends and means through the eyes of faith. Your end is to love God in your neighbor through Christ. Your means are those organizations and structures with which you try to serve humanity, cooperating sincerely and without manipulation. You love, rather than hate; you do not take advantage of others; you do not rebel.

626. You must choose a path of dedication which takes into account your abilities, the needs of your neighbor, and the circumstances in which you find yourself. You cannot do everything, but you do what you can well because you are doing it with faith.

627. Although being an apostle means following a path of wholehearted service in apostolic activities of a religious nature, this dedication does not lessen your obligation also to serve your neighbor in the secular circumstances in which Divine Providence has placed you.

628. If you lead a life of faith, you will look on things through the eyes of Jesus Christ and will be able to see the eternal dimensions.

629. When reading or listening to the news, you have to look beyond its human and historical aspects and be convinced that "This is the news of the kingdom of heaven." Then, after you have folded your newspaper and turned off your radio or television, you must pray fervently, "Thy kingdom come."

630. Behind the lines of newsprint or the sound-bites on the television screen you must discover the gospel values of the events reported. You should experience joy and hope in events which are advantageous to as well as sorrow and anxiety at those which hinder the progress of the people of God to the promised land.

631. We use various technical terms to distinguish between the spiritual and temporal realms, between the soul and the body. In the end, however, these elements cannot be separated from each other; they are bound up together in the heart of the child of God whose life and salvation history are one.

632. The secret of understanding events in our world is very simple. Use the gospel to nourish your soul. Once you are united with Christ, you will share in his Spirit which leads you to ask, "How does God look at the world?" The answer is at the center of our faith: "For God so loved the world that he gave his only Son, that whoever believes in him should not perish but have eternal life" (John 3:16).

633. Remember: You are carrying out God's plan in history every moment of your life.

Twenty-Seven: Renewal

Prepare for a new Pentecost in the Church.

634. Renewal means a return to the sources. The purpose of renewal in the Church is to help Catholics to return to a truly Catholic Church and for all Christians to return to Christ. This definition may surprise you, but upon reflection, you will recognize its validity. Gandhi often repeated a thought-provoking assertion which you would do well to remember: "I love Christ, but I do not like Christians because they are not Christlike."

635. Renewal is not defined by the changing of the external trappings of rituals to make them more attractive, changing the names of a few offices to render them more accessible, destroying old structures to make room for newer ones, or holding endless meetings to write endless manifestos. Renewal was better defined by St. Paul: "Put off your old nature which belongs

to your former manner of life and is corrupt through deceitful lusts, and be renewed in the spirit of your minds, and put on the new nature, created after the likeness of God in true righteousness and holiness" (Ephesians 4:22–24).

636. People today accuse the Church of being slow to move, old-fashioned, and weighed down by antiquated structures. It is no wonder, they argue, that it is in crisis. These poor people are mistaken; do not follow their example. Accusing the Church excuses no one from self-examination. After all, the Church is the People of God, of whom you are one. However, if there is a crisis, its causes are:

1) A devaluation and de-emphasis of prayer.
2) The loss by many Christians of a sense of the supernatural: they are now impossible to distinguish from others in society.
3) A reluctance to accept the "folly" of the Cross.

637. During the past few decades, people have consumed too much paper and ink writing about the need to "return to the sources." Talk is superfluous; you must act. What did the first Christians do? They were strongly motivated by the love of Christ which was always fresh in the minds. It was a revolution of love which reformed the Greco-Roman world, transforming its very foundations and stripping away the old human nature to make room for a new humanity and a new society.

638. Human love is limited to one group of people . . . spiritual love embraces all.

Human love returns love for love . . . spiritual love volunteers to risk the initiative of loving first.

Human love is drawn into itself . . . spiritual love unites with others.

Human love only touches humankind . . . spiritual love transforms humanity.

And once human beings are changed, society will change, laws will change, communications between people will change. This is total renewal.

639. In order to renew, you must return to the ultimate source, God. And what do the Scriptures tell us about God? St. John tells us that "God is love" (1 John 4:8). Jesus said that "I and the Father are one" (John 10:30).

Jesus wants our renewal to be according to his will: "A new commandment I give to you: that you love one another; even as I have loved you, that you also love one another" (John 13:34), and "that they may all be one; even as thou, Father, art in me, and I in thee" (John 17:21). Love and unity are the wellsprings of renewal!

640. How long will we have to be engaged in renewal? We must constantly begin again, always aiming at conversion. You can never be content if you have not made progress since yesterday in your unity with God; in fact, you can be sure that the moment you stand still is the moment you begin to slide backwards.

641. To what degree must you renew yourself? I want you to renew yourself to the degree of Christ's perfection. That is, you

must reach for a standard which cannot be improved, a standard whose sole measure is Christ Jesus.

642. In your self-renewal, be generous *toward* God and give completely whatever he desires of you. But do not forget the other side of this: Accept completely whatever he sends you.

643. Just as a sick child is restored to health by a transfusion of blood from its parents, your life and that of the Church is sustained by a continual outpouring of the blood of the Lord.

644. The press is never tired of emphasizing the sensational events and upheavals of the world. You should take note of these and share in the anxieties of humanity. But make constructive use of these stories. Let them urge you on to the building of a new world where the press will not find such stories to report. You must struggle to build the kingdom of God in this world with whatever means are at hand.

645. Every century experiences firsthand the Good News through the lives of those people whom Divine Providence bestows on the world: Augustine, Benedict, Bernard, Francis of Assisi, Vincent, Teresa of Avila, Ignatius of Loyola, John Bosco, Thérèse of Lisieux, and others throughout history. Each one of these individuals has stressed a new aspect of the gospel and introduced a new way of living it, which corresponded with the needs of the world during their particular periods.

646. Every day re-evangelize your mind through reading and

meditation. Immerse yourself in the everlasting word so that the gospel will gradually permeate and take root in every fiber of your existence. This is renewal, the most enduring revolution.

647. What is to become of our attempts at renewal—all our organizations and committees, all our sacrifices and actions? In a wider context, what is to become of modern man with all his machines, industries, and scientific achievements? What direction are we to take?

648. If we do not lift up our gaze to God for the hope, meaning, and consolation of our life, who will be able to explain it to us?

649. From this day forward, through your expression, your gestures, your silence, your heart, your soul, your actions, your very manner of living and dying, you must always radiate the light of the presence within you on to all the places you go and all the people you meet.

650. You are not renewed if you simply "keep the faith." Remember, the devil is constantly trying to drive God from the world and to drag it away from God. You, in turn, must bring God into the world and lead it to him.

651. Some people will die for the sake of an ideal. Every Christian who wants to serve humanity must live one ideal, God.

652. The most solid barrier is not a fortress or an electric fence. Rather, it is the barrier of indifference. Others may suffer or die

from hunger and poverty, but you are unaffected. Likewise, you are unconcerned about the decadence and collapse of civilization. With such an attitude, how are you ever going to be able to overcome the barrier of indifference?

653. The renewal of society will be accomplished by those people who faithfully renew themselves according to the gospel. Faith will give a new value to their work. People may not recognize them and some may never hear them speak, but everyone will perceive the difference as they see evidence of a more beautiful way of life.

654. You will not go far by rushing ahead quickly. Rather, you will advance further by walking firmly and purposefully. There is no need to make urgent appeals for the world to advance. Concentrate on beginning to advance yourself.

655. As Pope Paul VI pointed out repeatedly, if the world is to be renewed, it will be necessary to eliminate:

1) Secularism, because its ultimate aim is to look only to worldly happiness, and so it stands for hedonism, possessions, power, and influence.
2) A worldliness which no longer recognizes the values of sacrifice, humility, and patience.
3) Politicization which believes that only politics can solve the problems of peace, development, families, brotherhood, and justice.

656. Is your life a mere continuous chain of events? There is a time for sleeping, a time for waking, a time for eating, a time for studying, a time for working, a time for relaxation, a time for television, a time to read newspapers—but where is the unifying element of your life? Without an element of unity, something essential, unique, life would be truly boring and meaningless. In your life, this element should be the love of God. This love will change your life: All your actions will testify to God's presence within you.

657. Cooperate with others to bring about a new spring in the Church. Prepare people to welcome a new Pentecost. Become that open door which permits the cool breeze to enter and renew the Church.

658. If you are not advancing along the Road of Hope, if you are not aiming at holiness, you belong to neither the younger nor the older generations: You belong to the generation of the dead. Yet out of this age of vice, God can bring about an age of saints if you desire it in your life.

659. Renewal demands courage and determination. Called by God, in the face of so much suffering, do not be indifferent, pretending that you neither see the suffering nor hear the call. Be a dedicated disciple of the work of renewal and, with patient self-sacrifice, a lover of the Church.

660. The driving force and author of all the Church's renewal is the Holy Spirit, who "reneweth the face of the ground" (Psalm

104:30). True renewal is a new Pentecost, and there can be no Pentecost without the Holy Spirit. Always remember, you can renew nothing without the Holy Spirit.

661. Prepare yourself! You must strive unceasingly to announce effectively the Good News to the entire world, bringing your witness into every heart and family.

662. One dimension of renewal involves making the gospel relevant to the world of today. The Church cannot dilute the gospel, but it can present it to people today in a contemporary language. If the Church does not seek the people, they certainly will not seek it.

663. Do you pay attention to the world or do you lock yourself up in your little ghetto? Are you patiently helping to build a new society, brick by brick, or are you still following the old road of negative criticism?

Twenty-Eight: New Life

*Christians should not be downcast
like people without hope.*

664. People who have either lost their way or have never had any
way tend to lose hope. Such is not the case with the Christian
who is making progress *toward* his goal, because he has the certain hope of finding God, his loving Father, awaiting him there
where all his hopes and desires will be fulfilled.

665. For the person who knows nothing of an eternal goal, the
hour of death is a time of hopelessness and depression: It will
mean the loss of wealth, pleasure, and friends. All that lies before him is darkness, emptiness, loneliness. In contrast, for the
believer, the end of the Road of Hope is bathed in light.

666. Think for a moment about the drops of rain falling on a
winter's afternoon—there are so many that you scarcely notice

any one in particular. Every day, just as many people enter into eternity with hardly anyone taking notice. One day, you yourself will be among them.

667. While others may have regrets and complain about the end of life, you, on the contrary, are eager to proclaim your joyful hope in the coming of our Lord Jesus Christ.

668. Worldly people may say, "Every day brings me closer to the grave." You, however, should reply, "Every day brings me closer to the gates of heaven."

669. What worldly people regard as death, you should consider life, and what they call the "last breath," you should term the "first breath of new life," because what is for them an end is for you a new beginning.

670. Always be prepared, holding tightly the lamp of faith which has been entrusted to you and awaiting the day of the Lord's return—however, wherever, whenever he wishes.

671. When a child, temporarily left with a babysitter, hears its parents coming to retrieve it, it drops everything without so much as a thought and runs to meet them. In the same way, we should always be prepared to detach ourselves from this temporary abode on earth and return to our heavenly Father.

672. Knowing, as you do, that this earth is a temporary abode, how can you insist on placing such importance on this or that person,

place, or thing? Do you plan to take them with you to enjoy in heaven? How absurd it is even to contemplate such a thought!

673. We conclude many of our prayers with the phrase "who lives and reigns . . . for ever and ever. Amen." I am afraid that many Christians have dulled their ears to the eternal significance of these beautiful words. Yet what hope they contain!

674. In the face of innumerable trials and tribulations of this world, repeat to yourself with all your heart the words of The Apostles' Creed: "I believe in the resurrection of the body and the life everlasting." In these few words lies the secret of the Christian's courage and strength.

675. From the fate of so many women who were thought to be "beautiful"—stars, beauty queens, and the like—whose bodies have gradually come to know decay and corruption, you should grasp some idea of "nothingness." Draw your own conclusions.

676. Do not be so foolish as to leave to your last moments the task of regretting a life spent exchanging true riches for false imitations.

677. Even when they reached heaven, the apostles continued to assist the world. In fact, they now do more since their work is no longer hampered by the physical constraints of this life.

678. Apostles do not die; their life "is changed, not ended" (Preface I for the Dead). Remember: "Now we see in a mirror dimly; but then face to face" (1 Corinthians 13:12).

679. In the midst of all the hardships, deceptions, injustices, and persecutions you may suffer, stand firm with the whole People of God in affirming that: "He will come again in glory to judge the living and the dead, and his kingdom will have no end" (The Nicene Creed).

680. You should feel comforted that your judge is also your merciful Father. In fact, the more just he is, the more reassured you should be, since he will take into account your human frailties. But do not abuse his goodness by foolishly remaining in sin.

681. God has called you to be a saint. If you choose to go to hell, you show no gratitude for his love.

682. Faced with the most terrible trials, remember the promise of the Book of Revelation: "He will wipe away every tear from their eyes, and death shall be no more, neither shall there be mourning nor crying nor pain any more, for the former things have passed away" (Revelation 21:4).

683. At Fatima, Lucia, Jacinta, and Francisco were filled with fear and terror after their vision of hell. Nothing could erase the horror of the spectacle from their memories. Believe Mary's warning. Do not blind yourself to the existence of hell only to wake up one day and find yourself there.

684. For you, the most relevant new idea should be "eternity." Use it to make the most important decision of your life: Will it be an eternity of love in heaven or an eternity of hatred in hell?

685. The attitude of the early Christians when faced with death was completely new to their age. Their steadfast witness converted the Roman world to the belief in God and his eternal love.

686. The realization that this life is transient should not cause you to fall into escapism, pessimism, or neglect of duties. Rather, it should spur you on to compete enthusiastically against time. While others can say, "Time is money," you must believe that time is heaven and time is love.

687. Anything that does not bear the trademark "Eternity" is counterfeit.

688. The grain of rice sown in the paddy is not dead; from there it will rise to a new and more abundant life. Likewise, the grain of rice which is cooked does not die; it becomes food for humanity, living out a different, beautiful, and nobler life.

689. In the future, on those wreaths with which you honor the dead, do not put "With sincere sympathy." Similarly, stop referring to the dead as "deceased." Their bodies are simply resting in the hope of rising again, while their souls currently enjoy the beatific vision of God.

690. With Christians, there are no dead; all those among us who have died are living as members of Christ, just as much as we are. We remain united with each other through faith.

Twenty-Nine: Suffering

*If you constantly seek to avoid suffering,
do not expect to become a saint.*

691. The storms which blow past will sweep away dry and rotten branches, but they can never uproot the cross planted deep in the earth. Do not regret the loss of those dead branches; even if no wind had come by, they would have fallen by themselves or been cut away since their presence is harmful to the entire tree.

692. During his life on earth no matter where he went, Jesus encountered both those who were willing to live and die for him and those who were determined to kill him. Why then should you expect everyone to love you? Why are you so easily discouraged when you meet someone who hates you?

693. Along this road you are traveling, you will encounter thorns and brambles, tigers and other wild animals, as well as fragrant

roses and beautiful views. There will be kind friends and treach-erous enemies, times of soft rainfall and times of scorching sun. Be ready for both the pleasant and the unpleasant. Whatever comes, keep going forward, filled with the spirit of the Lord like Cyril and Athanasius: Do not stop, do not hesitate for fear of criticism, do not search for praise.

694. When you feel overwhelmed by suffering, look up to the cross, embrace it, and cling quietly and steadfastly beneath it with Mary.

695. In the midst of your trials, consider how little these suffer-ings are in comparison with the joys of heaven. Remember the divine perspective: "Blessed are the poor in spirit . . . those who mourn . . . those who are persecuted . . . for theirs is the kingdom of heaven" (Matthew 5:3–10).

696. You complain that others are ungrateful. Did you do them a favor only for the sake of being thanked?

697. You complain that your opponents are constantly disput-ing with you and obstructing your apostolic work. Have you forgotten the parable of the wheat and the weeds (see Matthew 13:24–30)? The wheat of your good works will continue to grow despite these obstacles.

698. You find your activity curtailed and your reputation ma-ligned as opposition builds on all sides. Wait for God's time

and remember that "every branch of mine that bears no fruit, he takes away, and every branch that does bear fruit he prunes, that it may bear more fruit" (John 15:2). The green branches will come to blossom again, bringing forth an even more abundant harvest.

699. Jesus shared his agony in the garden with the three disciples with whom he had a special bond of affection: Peter, James, and John. Are you afraid to be among his closest friends?

700. In times of suffering, avoid asking who was at fault, but rather simply give thanks to God for the instrument he uses to sanctify you. Also, avoid seeking merely human consolation; take your problems to Jesus in the Sacrament and to Mary. Then when the suffering has passed, resist any impulse to recrimination and vengeance. Forget about it, never speak about it again except to say "Alleluia!"

701. You are frustrated because you find it impossible to reason with your enemies. Do not be surprised: "So they persecuted the prophets who were before you" (Matthew 5:12).

702. If you expect to avoid suffering, do not expect to become a saint.

703. God uses trials and sufferings to teach us understanding and compassion for the sufferings of others. Remember, Jesus himself prayed for humanity, weeping heartfelt tears over it.

704. In heaven, will you say with regret, "How I wish I had had more opportunities to love God and to suffer for him!"

705. You suffer most when you suffer at the hands of those whom you expected to understand and sympathize with you, those who in fact ought to defend you. When this happens unite yourself with Jesus who, seemingly alone in his sufferings on the cross, cried out: "My God, my God, why hast thou forsaken me?" (Matthew 27:46).

706. United with the passion of Jesus, you will find your courage and patience strengthened and your sufferings will have considerable redemptive value.

707. If you feel tense, rest for a while: You will be more effective if you rebuild your strength. To accept that there are limits to your strength is a sign of courage and to know how to look after your health is a sign of wisdom.

708. While time is an important factor, you should not be hasty in your reactions. Rather, wait and consider things patiently. Often, after a night's rest, you will see things more clearly and objectively.

709. I once heard a doctor say, "Even if I were to be offered a thousand dollars a day, I would not want to nurse these sick people." He was gently, but quickly, rebuked by a young sister who observed, "As for me, doctor, neither would I were it not for the

love of God—even if I were offered your thousand dollars. But for God, I will stay here until death."

710. Suffering is the lot of humankind. However, for Christians, their lives should both proclaim the Lord's death and profess his resurrection.

711. Do good, but do not publish it abroad.

712. You are furious over some incident; it truly breaks your heart to have to bear injustice. However, consider this in the light of what the Lord suffered: What sins did Jesus commit to deserve crucifixion? Do you think he was treated fairly?

713. The rose and the lily will continue to bloom into beautiful, sweet-scented, and colorful flowers only so long as there is fertilizer which decays to feed them. Likewise, apostolic work flowers when it is nourished by suffering transformed into love.

714. The trials of suffering are the only way to follow the Lord into eternal happiness with him. Remember, "If any man would come after me, let him deny his own self and take up his cross, and follow me" (Matthew 16:24).

715. There is no suffering to compare with that of Jesus on the cross. As he was at the point of breathing his last, Jesus felt in the very depths of his soul the full weight of abandonment, the crushing burden of this great ignominy, which led him to cry

out, "My God, my God, why hast thou forsaken me?" (Matthew 27:46). During those terrible, dark moments in your own life, unite yourself with this suffering Jesus. You will be at peace and will have the strength to say with him finally, "Father, into thy hands I commit my spirit!" (Luke 23:46).

716. Jesus has asked us, "Are you able to drink the cup that I drink or to be baptized with the baptism with which I am baptized?" (Mark 10:38). As Christians, our response must be, "We will freely drink of this bitter cup because it is your bitter cup and because you, O Lord, have drunk of it for us!" The more bitter and full you find the cup, the greater will be your witness of love. And the more Jesus loves and trusts you, the more he will want to share his cup with you.

717. Suffering is a great burden if, out of fear, you seek to avoid it. However, suffering is a sweet experience if, out of love, you courageously accept it.

Thirty: A Happy Child

The condition of entry into heaven:
"Become like children" (Matthew 18:3).

718. While an orphan who has everything can be a happy person, despite his riches he can never know the happiness enjoyed by a child who has parents. Yet a poor child, provided he has loving parents, can be a happy person in spite of his poverty. No matter who or what you are, do you realize that you are the happiest of children because you are a child of God the Father and have the Virgin Mary for your mother?

719. Adults often tend to make rather complicated self-introductions which state their entire personal histories. A little child, in contrast, has a very simple method: It declares, "I am the child of Mr. and Mrs. So-and-so and we live at such-and-such a place." Be proud of your ability to identify yourself

easily in the manner of the little child: "I am a child of God and a child of Mary."

720. A little child once went to a shop to buy something for its mother, only to find the store was already closed. It knocked and knocked on the door until the shopkeeper finally opened it to scold whoever was causing the disturbance. However, when he saw the small child, so innocent and so simple, standing there, he could not find his angry words. Rather, full of smiles, he embraced the child, asking, "You poor little thing, what are you doing out at this hour?" The little child eventually got what he wanted. In your prayer, be like that little child.

721. A child does not need to know whether its parents are rich or poor; it only knows that it has a mother and father and that is enough to satisfy it. Even if a bomb drops on its house, while the child may experience some danger or suffering, it will still fall asleep peacefully if its parents are there to comfort it. The child dwells perpetually secure in the belief of the all-powerful love of its parents. Your trust in God's all-powerful love must be likewise.

722. No matter how many times a child makes the same mistake, its parents will still love it because they know it means no harm. Although they keep trying to do their best, things will still occasionally go wrong for children. But this does not matter; only their good will is of consequence. Likewise, God only asks for our good intentions. His grace will do the rest.

723. When you pray, do not worry about how you will go about asking God for what you want. Just keep your prayers simple and sincere like the requests made by a small child to its parents. Such a child knows that it is loved by its parents and will freely thrust its hand into its father's pocket or look into its mother's handbag searching for the treat it knows is there.

724. You are tired, you cannot concentrate, you feel discouraged. Never mind. So long as you love God, that is sufficient. After expending all of its energies at play, a tired child will cuddle in the arms of its parents and rest secure.

725. When a child accidentally breaks some object around the house, it does not attempt to avoid its parents or to act deceitfully. On the contrary, it runs crying to its parents to confess its wrongdoing. In turn, its parents, rather than mourn the loss of the object, will embrace the child to comfort it and soothe its worry. They value their child more than any material possessions they may have lost. In just the same way, you should be humble and sincere before God our Father, trusting in his understanding.

726. The parents ask their child for a sweet, but it withdraws and refuses to give them any. But when they insist, it begins to feel sorry and gradually opens its hand. The parents are overjoyed and give the child even more sweets because they did not really want its sweets originally, but to teach it to conquer its selfishness. God our Father likewise rejoices in our little sacrifices.

727. The spiritual life of a child of God is neither weak nor passive. Rather, it follows a spiritual road which is easy amid difficulties, simple in complexities, gentle but determined, powerful in its weakness, and wise in its foolishness.

728. The heart of a little child knows neither hatred nor indignation. It will cry when it is chastised by its parents, but it will soon enough forget this discomfiture and will even doze off in those very arms which have just chastised it. Learn from this example and put aside all your anger and animosity. Dwell in the arms of your heavenly Father and you will always be happy.

729. Have no fear about your inabilities, because it is the grace of God which will make a saint of you. Joyfully accept his will, being always prepared to follow lovingly wherever he leads you. Be fearless like the child who would be willing to go anywhere, even to the moon, provided its parents went with it.

730. When we speak of having the heart of a child, we mean neither a childish nor a naive heart. What we mean is having a love that is unlimited in its trust of our heavenly Father, willing to do everything that is asked of us with complete confidence. Be courageous and steadfast in a manner worthy of a child of God and of Mary.

731. Little children do not keep things for themselves, but rather hand everything over to their parents to keep and carry. Likewise, hand over everything in trust to God and to Mary, and you will always be happy and secure.

732. Some of your greatest deeds may not amount to as worthy an offering to almighty God as do some of your simplest tasks. This is because God sees your heart and loves you in a way similar to the love of parents who rejoice more over the first steps of their child than over the races it may run later in life.

733. Your strength on this Road of Hope comes from Jesus in the Sacrament and from Mary.

734. Time belongs to God, all creation is his, he is the Alpha and the Omega, the beginning and the end. God is omnipotent and Lord of all: He takes care of the birds of the air, the fish of the sea, and the creatures of the land and the flowers of the field. Despite this, he counts every hair on your head because he is concerned only with love. Peace and happiness to the humble, childlike soul which longs for this eternal love!

735. Our conception of the way to heaven is often complicated and difficult. But Jesus laid down only one condition: "Truly I say to you, unless you turn and become like children, you will never enter the kingdom of heaven" (Matthew 18:3).

736. Confide everything into God's hands and then stop being afraid. There is nothing hard about this! Although you may not know where he is leading you (and you can be sure that there will be surprises along the way), it is enough that you should believe that God is your Father.

Thirty-One: Charity

Charity is the signature of a Christian.

737. Before making any decisions about how you should act in a particular case, pray. Then do what Jesus would do in the same circumstances.

738. Just because you busy yourself about some task in a far-off place, you are not necessarily practicing charity. Only when you settle down to undertake the same work with the same ardor in your own neighborhood, among those who come into daily contact with you, will I believe that you are practicing true charity.

739. Complaining is a contagious disease whose symptoms are pessimism, loss of peace, doubts, and a decrease in the zeal which comes from close union with God.

740. Making a donation, buying a raffle ticket, and giving away old clothes are easy enough. Often, these are acts performed more to avoid being disturbed further, rather than as true acts of charity. Only love is difficult. Therefore next time leave your love in the book which records your donation, in the raffle ticket, and in that bag of old clothes.

741. You excuse yourself saying, "I cannot perform acts of charity because I have no money." Why do you think you need money to practice charity? What about the charity of a smile and a warm handshake, the charity of human compassion and understanding, the charity of a visit or a remembrance in your prayers?

742. Do not wait until you are about to die to make peace with each other. Do not delay giving away your possessions until you are near death and no longer have use for them. An act of charity that cannot be avoided or that is only reluctantly performed brings only regrets because it lacks the fundamental ingredient of love.

743. Other people do not need your help or your possessions as much as they need your love.

744. Do not become angry when you are criticized by other people. Rather, you should be grateful that they do not mention all your faults.

745. Few things are as beautiful as people living together in the spirit of fraternity. Jesus himself declared that, "Where two

or three are gathered in my name, there am I in the midst of them" (Matthew 18:20). He knew this would not be easy, so he demanded only a bare minimum from you: He does not ask for many more than "two or three."

746. Living in fraternity both tests and supports the spirit of charity. Remember the trees of the forest which support one another against being blown down during tempests.

747. A drunkard never really knows with certainty to what extent he will cause damage, whether by stabbings, murder, or arson. In a like manner but worse, when you are seething with revenge, you suffer an even greater loss of your powers of perception.

748. Jesus commanded his disciples to wear a simple uniform, but it was a difficult one to find: "By this all men will know that you are my disciples, if you have love for one another" (John 13:35).

749. Wherever there is love, there God is present. Wherever there is hatred, there is hell.

750. If your only motive for helping and counseling your neighbors is to learn more about them, your charity is that of a secret agent.

751. In the space of a few seconds, anybody can deface one of Raphael's paintings which took him months to complete. Even more tragic, who would ever be able to duplicate what Raphael

had done? Likewise, a person's reputation can be destroyed forever by the careless tongues of others.

752. Jesus said, "If you are offering your gift at the altar and there remember that your brother has something against you, leave your gift there before the altar and go; first be reconciled to your brother and then come and offer your gift" (Matthew 5:23–24). Instead you do the opposite: You offer your gift while you continue to air your grievance to everyone except the person concerned. Such is your version of the good news!

753. You continually call for dialogue while refusing to allow anyone to express ideas contrary to your own fixed notions. This kind of dialogue is hampered by its own limits and by a prearranged program—or, rather, we have two monologues instead of a dialogue.

754. It would be absurd if a laborer criticized the instructions of an engineer on building a bridge or those of an architect on building a house. Likewise it could be unacceptable for a hospital porter to question the directions of a surgeon. Why then do you criticize your superiors who have more reasons, more competence, and more help from the grace of God on which to base their considerations than you would have?

755. Love others not with words, but with actions. Love with your right hand without letting your left hand know. "Love one another as I have loved you."

756. There are many kinds of charity:

- the noisy kind, like the charity of self-servers who brag of their "good works";
- the self-publicizing kind, like the charity of banks;
- the feeding kind, like the charity of zoos;
- the downward-looking kind, like the charity of snobs;
- the opinion-oriented kind, like the charity of dictators;
- the exhibitionist kind, like the charity of frauds.

757. The unjust word of a just man can do endless damage. It is like a poison dispensed by a doctor: the more reputable its source, the more it will be spread about and the more people it will kill.

758. People leading the religious life have only one possession which they can truly call their own: their reputation. Therefore, anyone who violates this sacred possession is guilty of assassination.

759. If you praise only those who praise you, accept only those who do not oppose you, and keep company only with those who share your opinions, you have neither charity nor wisdom. Your conduct is simply another case of the blind leading the blind.

760. In a community in which there is an extremist, even a religious one, that person will often be the unwitting cause for the making of many martyrs.

761. If you would put yourself in the place of others, you would soon realize how careless and irresponsible your public statements have been and you would quickly learn to exercise greater prudence.

762. Things are always easier said than done. All are quick to deplore the present, yearn for the past, and applaud their own schemes for the future. But, when that future becomes the present, woe to anyone else who criticizes it!

763. What kind of logic is this? You call your own bad temper a virtue while terming your neighbor's good will a fault.

764. Why are you so busy attacking your neighbors when there is no shortage of defects in your own character?

765. Your love for your neighbor is the most reliable test of your love for God.

766. Loving others does not mean that you have to lavish signs of affection on them or spoil them in any way. In fact, loving them may occasionally mean you must cause them some discomfort for the sake of truth or for their own good.

767. Jesus did not teach us to love according to our subjective emotions since he commanded us to love even our enemies. Loving others means sincerely to wish them well and to do everything in our power to help them to secure their happiness. This requires that we forget ourselves completely.

768. You must become like a gift in the hand of God, prepared to be presented by him to one and all without distinction. Such a gift is desired and loved by all.

769. The biggest mistake is not to be aware that other people are Christ. There are many people who fail to discover this truth until the Day of Judgment.

770. If you were to examine the personalities of each person, you would discover that no two are the same. Human personality is not like a cassette tape or a stereo record which can be mass-produced. So never generalize judgments.

771. We must learn always to thank each other: the recipient, because he has received the love and assistance he needed, and the donor, because he has been given an opportunity to grow in love.

772. Why do you set up a court which your neighbors must pass through daily? Why do I always see you on the judge's bench and never in the dock?

773. Replace your diplomatic grin with a sincere Christian smile.

774. Charitable and social works are both necessary and beneficial. In this modern age, however, we cannot say that we love truly unless we are dedicated to demanding changes in the structures and personnel that prevent authentic human liberation and which are obstacles to humanity living more humanly.

775. It would be so wonderful if God required us only to love him. However, he has chosen also to require the difficult obligation to love our neighbor, a requisite just as important as the first even if not as easy.

776. Why do you chisel the shortcomings of others into rock while recording your own sins on the sands?

777. The circumstances in which you find yourself may curtail your activity; nevertheless, remain committed to spreading love in whatever way you can in that ambiance. One day, when you look again over those places through which you have passed, you will be surprised to learn that the seeds of love which you sowed have grown ten or a hundredfold among those Divine Providence destined you to meet along the Road of Hope.

778. What is a blessing for a community? It is "Blessed are those who are persecuted for righteousness' sake" (Matthew 5:10). Yes, this is truly the way it is. I am referring specifically to those systematically planned and executed persecutions which this age has known all too well. Such persecutions bring redemption because they place you in an historic role within the Church's mission to change the world.

779. A true community is a united body and does not treat its members as mere units, but rather as individual human beings.

780. Formerly, religious life consisted almost exclusively of fasting, rising early in the morning, staying up late at night,

and leading a life of silence. Today, however, religious life also consists of living together in community, meeting to exchange views with one another, and working together for the common good of society.

781. Every night before you go to bed, you should be able to say with honesty, "I have loved all day today."

782. Anyone who makes false accusations against another person, reviling them and stirring up hatred and opposition, for whatever reason, cannot hide his contradiction of the gospel, because "God is love" (1 John 4:8).

783. Calmly take a sheet of paper and honestly write down the virtues of the people whom you dislike. You will find that these people are not as bad as you had thought them to be.

784. Why do you complain that other people are ungrateful to you? Do you fear that your work will go unrewarded? Remember, "As you did it to one of the least of these my brethren, you did it to me" (Matthew 25:40).

785. Why are you so sparing in your praise of others, so slow to smile or to shake a hand? There are so many people in the world who want neither your money nor your possessions. They need only your heart.

786. Unless your charitable works are done for God, you are no more than a salaried social worker.

787. Charity knows no boundaries: If there are boundaries, it is no longer charity.

788. Whenever you help anyone, make sure that you are practicing charity with all your heart so that the recipient of your good works may forgive you for the uneasiness which he feels on these occasions.

789. Whenever Jesus performed a miracle for anyone, he usually ordered the person to keep it quiet. On the other hand, there are many people who have never performed a miracle and yet they go about telling everyone how charitable they are.

790. Do not complain that your coffee is bitter; it is only because your sugar is not sweet enough.

791. A machine, regardless of how well-built it is, will break down if its mechanical parts are not kept well-oiled. In your life, pour the oil of charity on all your actions and everything will go smoothly for you.

792. Charity is an extension of the love of God for humanity.

793. As a Christian, you should be able to say sincerely, "I do not regard anyone as my enemy, not even those who hate me the most or who persecute me or who desire only my destruction. I look upon everyone as I would look upon my own brothers and sisters."

794. If you are good, but others call you bad, you are still good. And if you are poor, but others praise you for being rich, you are still poor. So why are you so concerned about what others think of you?

795. Some people engage in all kinds of self-publicity to flatter themselves about imagined talents, to spread propaganda about illusory achievements, or perhaps to blackmail their opponents with false accusations of evil-doing. They may even succeed in fooling some other people. But do you expect to hoodwink God in this way?

796. Monks and nuns are aided in their life of holiness by a variety of particular religious exercises: regulated fasting and self-denial, the Rule of their order or congregation, communal recollection, and so on. Laypeople have one principal means: to lead holy lives, they must practice charity.

797. Charity is the constant cultivation of the virtues connected with the heart, the mind, the temperament, the eyes, the ears, the tongue, and so on. Even if your whole being rebels against this discipline, your reaction must always be to do as Jesus would.

798. "In my Father's house are many rooms" (John 14:2). How penetrating is the word of God! Diversity! Treat everyone differently according to each individual's personality, something that must be respected. Do not look at everyone as if they were all the same: Human beings are not quantities or numbers. With

individuals, two plus two does not always equal four, just as with melons. Yes, melons. Two melons plus two melons generally adds up to four kilos, but sometimes you may need six melons to make up four kilos. The moral is, look at each case individually.

799. The practice of charity means that we strive to become a community which produces new relationships. If there are new relationships, there will be a new world.

800. Charity should lead to a new dimension of love and forgiveness which creates a new atmosphere in local, national, and international communities.

801. Charity is what differentiates the world of animals from the world of human beings, the world of the children of man from the world of the children of God.

802. It is not enough not to hate anyone. Neither is it sufficient just to love someone or just to help someone else. Only when we have love of others combined with action on their behalf do we begin to have enough. Remember the prayer of Jesus: "That they may all be one; even as thou, Father, art in me, and I in thee" (John 17:21).

803. Jesus suffered abandonment on the cross and continues to suffer it still in the person of every one of his brothers and sisters in agony anywhere in this world.

804. On the Last Day, the Lord will judge you on the basis of

your practice of the virtue of charity, not on any great successes you may have achieved.

805. Do not engage in that despicable habit of speaking ill of people who are not present. Speak as if your words were being recorded, act as if your actions were being filmed.

806. If you fail to carry out the last testament of Jesus— that is, to live a life in witness to charity—you will truly be a most ungrateful and unfortunate child of God.

Thirty-Two: Ordinary Work

Carry out your ordinary work in an extraordinary way.

807. Your work may be small and your heart small, or your work small and your heart big, or your work big and your heart small, or your work small and your heart big—these are all possibilities. I tell you, however, that you must be wholehearted in the least thing that you do. To be faithful in big things is easy, but to be faithful in little things can be quite difficult. That is why the Lord praised those who did so.

808. From the point of view of the world, there was nothing out of the ordinary about the things Mary did during her life: her help to her cousin Elizabeth, her care and concern for her infant son, her duties in the home at Nazareth, the journeys to worship at the Temple in Jerusalem, her burial of her husband Joseph, and her anguish at the sufferings of her son, Jesus. But from

a supernatural perspective, her life was extraordinary because everything she did, she did out of obedience to and love for God.

809. To carry a baby is a commonplace event, but when the baby is being carried about by its mother, it is an event marked by the greatest happiness for the baby which cannot be replaced by anything in the world.

810. "The guiding principle of my life has been to accept everything with a humble heart while thinking of a few ordinary ideas which will have great consequences" (Pope John XXIII).

811. There is no such thing as an unworthy work, only an unworthy heart.

812. A noble heart can make even the most ordinary act an act of nobility.

813. In order to be canonized, a candidate must have his heroic virtues proven. To persevere in the fulfillment of our ordinary work throughout our lives for the love of God is certainly heroic; such was the way of St. Thérèse of the Child Jesus.

814. If you want to become a saint, do ordinary things well. Even if they seem insignificant, pour the love of your entire heart into them.

815. If you continue to look for big things while despising smaller things, you will surely lose your way along this Road of Hope.

816. Whenever you see an ancient tree, never forget that hundreds of years ago, it was just a tiny seed.

817. Can we reach the summits of the Himalayas by sheer magic? Can we get to the moon by simple desire? No. How many trials and dangers have to be overcome before we are even halfway there! We must diligently persevere each step of the way, each and every day.

818. You tell me that you are waiting for an "opportune moment" so that you may do something truly grand. But how do you know that such an occasion will ever simply present itself? Rather, seize the opportunities presented every day to carry out ordinary deeds in an extraordinary manner.

819. Among those who buy tickets to scale a Manhattan skyscraper and who praise the modernity of its construction, there are few who take the time to notice each piece of metal, each grain of sand that forms the foundation for the whole edifice.

820. Look down a microscope and notice how a drop of water can be more brilliant than a diamond and a microbe can look more terrifying than a monster. Do not underestimate small things.

821. A given task may seem unimportant but, because of the tears and sweat which are spent in its execution, it acquires a great value. A task may seem rather ordinary, but it becomes important because of the love which informs it. A loving child will continue to put on an old woolen sweater, and even refuse

a newer, more expensive, garment, because each thread in the sweater is a sign of its mother's love.

822. Your daily life is like a rosary in which the beads are the humble expressions of ordinary, daily life, held together by the chain of faith and charity.

823. A harmonious melody, a marvelous painting, and a beautiful tapestry, can be reduced to simple notes, strokes, or threads. But only a patient genius succeeds in turning these elements into a masterpiece.

824. The Lord used the five loaves of bread and two fish of a young boy to work the miracle of feeding the five thousand men, plus women and children (Matthew 14:17). The Lord may be all-powerful, but he depends on your cooperation.

825. The Samaritan woman whom he asked for a drink of water, the man from whom he borrowed an ass for the entry into Jerusalem, the fisherman from whom he borrowed the boat from which to preach to the crowds, the homeowner whose room was lent for the institution of the Eucharist, the widow whom he saw putting her last pennies in the temple treasure—these anonymous persons never imagined the prominent mention which they were to receive from the Lord (see John 4:7; Matthew 21:2–3; 26:18; Mark 12:43)!

826. The most insignificant gestures (those that cost nothing or require no great effort and generally pass unnoticed) can create

an inviting climate of love. Remember that the moon, despite its beauty, is inhospitable to life because it has no atmosphere.

827. Along the road of consecration, no act is mediocre: The smallest act of service to others is another step toward love. With this love grows your very being.

828. We know nothing of what the Holy Family did during the thirty years of hidden life in Nazareth. Only in heaven will we have any knowledge of their life there.

829. We can take it for granted that the thirty hidden years of the Lord's life were filled with love, harmony, and unity beyond human understanding because this is the mystery of God's love.

830. Thirty years of life, filled with their joys and sorrows, passed by. There must have been many moments of indescribable happiness as Jesus looked lovingly up to Mary and Joseph, and they looked with love on him. And the whole family must have looked up to God the Father with love. Theirs were years of great happiness amid the most common labors because those tasks were performed with the greatest spiritual unity.

831. If I should become a martyr and "deliver my body to be burned," if I were to become an apostle and preach "in the tongues of men and of angels," if I were to become a philanthropist and "give away all I have," but lack charity, "I gain nothing" (1 Corinthians 13:2–3). It is not so much what you do, but how you do it that matters.

832. At this very moment, you can do either your will or God's will. Which will it be?

Thirty-Three: Leadership

The leader is the one who willingly serves the others.

833. Travelers along the Road of Hope need a leader—literally, someone who will lead the way—a chief, a head. Without a head to think, the limbs of the body would go limp, good will would be stifled, and energy wasted, while chaos would dominate, turning the task at hand into ruin.

834. A leader is someone who knows, desires, and accomplishes a mission by inspiring others to know, desire, and accomplish that same mission.

835. A leader is one who serves. He is at the service of all, serving both God and those whom he leads. A true leader wants to be a servant.

836. Jesus came to cast fire on the earth and desired that it set the world aflame with a brilliant light (see Luke 12:49). You must be that bright flame of his, kindled with the fire of apostolic zeal. You must use your little fire to light still other torches until the whole world is a vast sea of living flames.

837. Should you find yourself chosen by God to be a leader in some particular circumstance, be humble and generous. You have been entrusted with a mission of supreme importance. Remember the joy and generosity of the apostles when they first heard the Lord's words: "Follow me and I will make you become fishers of men" (Mark 1:17).

838. You must believe in your mission. You must convert others to it as well, communicating your conviction and zeal to them.

839. If you cannot overcome that spirit of pessimism, that attitude of despondency, or that shy disposition, do not try to be a leader.

840. A leader is a visible sign of authority. He must always be mindful of his mission to command, his duty to exercise authority and to enable others to respect it. This is what is meant by serving other people as a leader.

841. The greatest failure in leadership is to have a leader who is afraid to speak and act like a leader.

842. Welcome all opinions, but do not depend on opinions.

843. Only those with effective initiative are fit to lead.

844. Bring all the faculties of your mind to bear on the formulation of a decision, then bring all your courage to bear on its execution at the opportune moment.

845. Your endless stream of opinions without resolution is useless. A true leader is a person who focuses on a few ideas, but nevertheless carries them out to the end.

846. Know what you want and desire it with your whole heart. If you lack this firm conviction, you will paralyze your followers. And if you allow them to make all the decisions for themselves, you will breed chaos.

847. The leader lives a life of discipline which seeks to understand the obligations of authority and then acts in accordance with them. The leader looks for ways to carry out plans and struggles valiantly against all obstacles which arise against them.

848. Public criticism of your superiors dampens zeal and creates division among your colleagues. Remember, such criticism opens the way for others to be critical of you and to find faults with your character.

849. There is no activity which does not involve carrying the cross. If you will not shoulder the cross, you will end up doing nothing.

850. If you want to be an effective leader, you will also need to learn how to rest. Knowing how to relax is essential if you are to avoid impetuousness, mental fatigue, moodiness, loss of self-control, and panic.

851. A leader must have courage; he needs to be calm in the face of unexpected events no matter when or where they arise. If he builds up these abilities, he will be able to overcome the most severe of trials successfully.

852. Overwork leads to an inability to achieve anything; anxiety can lead to insanity. No matter how busy you are, you must set aside time for reflection, study, and, most importantly, prayer. In fact, the busier you are, the more you need to reflect, study, and pray. In this way you will find peace.

853. Lose not a single moment, utter not a single superfluous word, waste not a single opportunity. If you act in this way, you will train your abilities and become even more determined, earning the respect and admiration of those whom you lead.

854. You must learn how to maintain personal discipline, organize your thoughts, and discern the value of every activity. These are the conditions required of a leader if he is to be able to fulfill his duty of restoring order and confidence when everyone is stricken by panic and fear.

855. See things the way they are: clearly and correctly. This is the

kind of realistic frame of mind you will need if you are to judge effectively the cases placed before you as a leader.

856. Set formulas are mechanical and mindless. It is useless and narrow-minded to be weighed down by rigid set procedures and lost in small details. Rather, you must take into account the general perspective, being flexible at all times and ever ready to change the bad into the good. You will need experts and advisers, and, most of all, your own resolute intentions.

857. You must nurture and cultivate your talents that you may serve more effectively.

858. If you are an incompetent leader, you will suffer not only loss of prestige, but also loss of credibility.

859. Do not expect your leader to possess every possible talent and ability, because you will never find such an ideal leader. If you yourself should be a leader, however, strive to develop your talents and abilities to the maximum of your potential.

860. In order to direct every activity and focus every effort on his goals, a leader must be able to discern general ideas. In this way, he will obtain a more complete understanding of all the workings of his organization.

861. Every individual is a unique mystery. If you are to be a leader, you must get to know all your followers and all their needs, desires,

and temperaments. You must be able to assess their interests and abilities in order to place them in exactly the right position.

862. Just as Jesus lived with his disciples for three years, you too must mix with your co-workers and followers. Be compassionate with them, sharing their confidences, joys, and sorrows, trying to understand each of them as an individual. If you do this, you will be surprised at the unity and excellence which you will have inspired.

863. Try placing yourself in the position of your subordinates. As a friend who exchanges views with them, treats them warmly, and allows them to see a genuine interest in their well-being, you will earn their love and confidence.

864. The medals pinned on your chest or the citations hung on your wall will not be your memorial as a leader. That is etched in the hearts and on the faces of your colleagues.

865. If you win the hearts of those under your authority, they will enthusiastically and devotedly follow you because they know that you love them deeply and are willing to make personal sacrifices for them. But, if you will not lead with love in this manner, you will have to employ the worst possible method: force.

866. To win the hearts of his fellows, a leader must dare to:

- be sure of his position and willing to allow others to share in the responsibilities;
- be humble while keeping in mind the dignity of his position;
- mix with his colleagues informally while retaining their respect;
- demand the complete obedience of all once he has made a decision.

867. Never forget that your co-workers are human, that they are individuals and children of God, who alone has absolute authority over them. Never think of them as mere possessions or productive machines.

868. A responsible leader will always work with a successor, whoever that may be, in mind. Strive for the permanence of your work, not the endurance of your reputation.

869. The leader whose actions contradict his words may be obeyed, but he is never respected. The leader whose accomplishments in office are exemplary may be respected, but not necessarily loved. But the leader who gives a shining example in every field, human and professional, will be obeyed, respected, and loved. His will be the most far-reaching influence.

870. The mark of a truly great leader is his ability to recruit co-workers by seeking them, discovering them, welcoming them, choosing them, training them, employing them, trusting them, and loving them. Nevertheless, keep in mind that there is no ideal leader any more than there is an ideal worker.

871. God must be the sole guide in all leadership. As the source of true leadership, he will not fail to support those whom he has chosen to share in his authority. Therefore, as the Gospels clearly show, true leadership is founded on a spirit of humility and charity.

872. A leader does not base his judgments on reports about his followers. Rather, he tries to know them personally, reading their hearts, learning their abilities, and sharing in their trials.

873. Jesus did not convert the apostles by issuing orders to them. Rather, he gave them time to change their hearts. Be self-confident in your mission and share that confidence with others. Live in such a way that they will gradually come to imitate you.

874. Jesus did not instruct his followers by setting up a school or writing a manual. He taught them to learn from real-life situations with lessons taken from the vineyard, the wheat field, the little children, and even from their own quarrels with each other.

875. Although Jesus used formal discourses to teach some specific truths, he seemed to prefer informal encounters. How much grace he poured out in such unexpected moments as the meetings with Zacchaeus, the Samaritan woman, and Simon of Cyrene!

876. Do not become discouraged with co-workers who may be unwilling or ungenerous, or who may even be malevolent or cruel. Remember, Jesus did not reject the apostles even when they

failed to understand or were even obstinate in their ignorance. Be patient and kind: God's grace will eventually win them over.

877. There are many families and communities who know only how to speak the language of the tongue to each other. If only they would learn the language of speaking heart to heart, they would be much more closely united.

878. When conversing with St. Peter, Jesus did not silence him because of his impetuosity. The angry outbursts of others will not cause the world to collapse. Do not be afraid: Continue speaking heart to heart instead of arguing with other people.

879. In the Gospels you will find the guiding principle for a dialogue in which the heart will be opened and liberated and the mind rendered wise and perceptive.

880. Jesus never refused anybody who wished to speak to him. He spoke freely with friends and strangers, Jews and Gentiles, saints and sinners, even his mortal enemies.

881. To be an effective leader, you must be all things to all people in all circumstances. Good leadership requires a readiness for every kind of work, for fatigue, opposition, and, if necessary, sacrifice, even of your own life, for the benefit of others. In all this, however, never forget your own spiritual needs.

882. When you assume the responsibilities of leadership keep this one fact in mind: Even after you have brought the task at

hand to a successful conclusion, you should still regard yourself as a useless servant, recognizing that you still have many faults and failings. With this in mind, do not be surprised if all your efforts meet only misunderstanding and ingratitude.

Thirty-Four: Examination
of Conscience

*We must continually review our lives
in the light of the gospel.*

883. While traveling on this Road of Hope, you will occasionally need to stop under the shade of a tree along the way to review your progress. Based on your experience so far, you may need to decide either to procure some extra provisions for the journey or to make some adjustments to your itinerary.

884. The greater the task before you, the more careful you must be with its planning. If you disregard this principle, you hold your eternal life in little esteem.

885. To look to the past and lament is useless.

To look to the past to take inordinate pride in accomplishments is dangerous.

To look to the past to learn its lessons for the present is the beginning of wisdom.

886. You must be thorough, sincere, and courageous in your examination of conscience. Just as you would not expect an accountant to have the results before conducting an audit, likewise when you conduct your examination allow the facts to speak for themselves and be ready to acknowledge your spiritual balance sheet as it really is.

887. Regardless of how well-built a car may be, it will still need periodic inspections. No matter how good your health appears to be, you still need regular medical checkups. It is the same with your soul. Therefore, thoroughly examine your conscience every night, every week, every time you approach the sacrament of reconciliation—indeed, every time you are recollected.

888. Do not overlook those "little" acts of unfaithfulness. Remember, storms and floods are not the only things which can destroy a crop; tiny insects can devastate a field overnight.

889. Only an extremely foolish soldier would be so occupied with trying to avoid a head wound that he turns his back on the enemy. Yet this is precisely how you are acting if you are so preoccupied with avoiding a mortal sin that you forget that gradual accumulation of venial sins.

890. You are rightly sorry for the many times you have betrayed the Lord. Sorrow, however, is not enough. You must be like Mary Magdalene whose "sins, which are many, are forgiven for she loved much" (Luke 7:47) and St. John who ran away from Jesus in the garden but returned to stand at the foot of the cross. Resolve always to love in deed as well as in word.

891. If you cannot try to avoid venial sins, your love of God is weak and you will not be able to persevere along the Road of Hope.

892. Failure to examine your conscience is a very serious matter: It indicates a tendency to sins of omission which can lead to an indifferent attitude toward God's will, a loss of the spirit of sacrifice, an avoidance of responsibility, an increase in worldliness, and an unwillingness to confront difficulties directly.

893. Your repentance and resolution of amendment should not resemble an actor in a Chinese opera who sheds copious tears during the performance only to revert to his jovial self the moment the curtain is lowered.

894. A spacecraft soars deep into space, but its flight path has been clearly predetermined and its pilot must constantly adjust the steering according to instructions communicated from mission control. If he does not, he and his craft may never reach their goal.

895. If you simply look at the engine of a malfunctioning motor car without making any of the necessary repairs, it will continue

to malfunction. Likewise, no matter how well you examine your conscience, unless you make firm resolutions to amend your life, the examination will be of no use to you.

896. When making your examination, concentrate on making practical resolutions. A thousand vague points will not add an iota to your holiness of life.

897. "Leave it till later" is occasionally the prudent policy of a wise person, but it is more often the lame excuse of a weak-willed procrastinator.

898. The present moment alone is important. Do not remember yesterday in order to weep over it: It is now in the past. Do not worry about tomorrow: It is still in the future. Entrust the past to God's mercy and the future to his providence. As to the present, strive to live it in his love.

899. When you fall short, do not become despondent. Do you think you belong to one of the nine choirs of angels and are incapable of committing a sin?

900. You have committed yourself to being an apostle, but you still do not entrust everything to the Lord. How do you expect to be an effective tool in his hands if you will not allow him control of the instrument?

901. Faced with a great responsibility, you feel tempted to rely on human machinations rather than the power of God, hoping

to obtain quick results. But are you undertaking this project for his glory or your own?

902. Are you afraid of being ridiculed by other people for being "naive"? Remember that Francis of Assisi, Teresa of Avila, Joseph Cottelengo, and John Bosco were all called mad while they lived, but now they are acclaimed as saints. Have confidence in God and continue to press forward.

903. If you are to head in the right direction on the Road of Hope, you must be able to say without hesitation: "Lord, all I do I do for love of you and for you in my neighbor. I will not hold back anything for myself. I do not ask to be thanked. I seek no reward."

904. After you have examined your conscience, what should you do? You must weep over your sins like Peter, lay yourself at his feet like Mary Magdalene, resolve to reform with the resolution of Zacchaeus and the zeal of Paul. Only in this way will you advance with hope.

905. Hope will remain only hope so long as you depend only on yourself. But when you allow your hopes and desires to be shaped by the grace of God, they will be realized in a way you could not even have imagined.

906. You have the following means at your disposal:

1) The Blessed Sacrament: "And lo, I am with you always, to the close of the age" (Matthew 28:20).

2) The Holy Spirit: "I will pray the Father, and he will give you another Counselor, to be with you for ever" (John 14:16).
3) Mary: "Behold, your mother!" (John 19:27)
4) The gospel: "Go into all the world and preach the gospel to the whole creation" (Mark 16:15).

Our Lord gave you all these, so why do you consider them of such little value? Does the world offer you anything which even compares with them?

907. Your plans are vast, your undertaking is enormous; and the obstacles you face seem as high as mountains and as vast as the sea. You begin to wonder how your frailness will ever surmount these difficulties. Take to heart the words of St. Paul: "God chose what is weak in the world to shame the strong" (1 Corinthians 1:27) and "By the grace of God I am what I am, and his grace toward me was not in vain" (1 Corinthians 15:10). All things are possible, provided you remain open and faithful to God's grace.

908. Examining your conscience means to review your life in the light of faith.

909. Every six months, take the time to draw up a summary of all your activities, an inventory of all your belongings, and a review of all changes in your sentiments. Submit these to a thorough judgment, having the courage to dispose of those things which are useless.

Thirty-Five: Our Mother Mary

Although she was poor, she gave us the greatest treasure: the Lord Jesus Christ, our Redeemer and the source of all graces.

910. No matter what someone may do to reassure a child, if its mother is not there, it will obstinately refuse to go along. Yet if its mother is there to hold its hand, a child will valiantly go through a forest, ford a stream, endure hunger and cold—clinging to its mother all along. Such is this bond that, during the war, I saw children who clung to their mothers' bodies, even after the mother had been killed. Along this Road of Hope, cling like a child on to the hand of our mother Mary and you will never be alone. She is "our life, our sweetness, and our hope."

911. Look at that child who wants its mother: It will continue sobbing until she returns. Even if you were to give it a sweet or a present of some kind, it would probably throw it away—nothing

will satisfy the child except the comforting presence of its mother. You must become like this child if you are truly to come to know and to love our mother Mary.

912. The love of Mary is like a cool breeze or a drop of morning dew: It brings refreshment and strength to the restless soul yearning for peace.

913. "Behold, your mother!" (John 19:27). After he gave us himself in the Eucharist, the Lord could offer us nothing greater than his beloved mother. She has crushed the head of the serpent under her foot. She will help us in our struggles against the devil, the flesh, and the world. She will obtain for us the favors we need to hold firm to the noble ideal Jesus has impressed within our hearts.

914. If a child is born ugly or crippled, its mother will nevertheless love it. No matter how badly you have fallen into sin, turn to Mary and entrust yourself to her. Jesus himself bequeathed her to us: "Behold, your mother!" (John 19:27). How could a mother abandon her child?

915. When you fall, weep humbly with her, because your falling has caused the death of her son. She will receive your sorrow. She accepted the good thief and Mary Magdalene as well as the beloved apostle John. She will likewise accept you as her child.

916. Mary is like a popular, pocket-sized book of the Gospels—more accessible to you than the lives of all the saints.

917. If you want to begin understanding what a wonderful mother you have, contemplate for a moment that she is the mother of the almighty Second Person of the Holy Trinity. You are indeed blessed that she is also your mother. It is so wonderful a mystery that you would never have known it unless Jesus himself had told you.

918. If you want to become a saint, be like a child. A child does not comprehend theories of behavior, but it does watch its mother and imitates her conduct, believing her to know everything and always to be correct. Therefore, look to our mother Mary and imitate her example and you will become a saint.

919. The Litany of the Blessed Virgin Mary is like a little guidebook with which the Church leads us to a deeper understanding and appreciation of the various attributes of our mother: powerful, merciful, amiable. The more you ponder these points, the more you will be filled with joy and hope amid your present struggles. And like a child, you will call on your mother: "Pray for us! Pray for us!"

920. The life of Mary can be summarized in three Latin words:
   Ecce . . . "Behold, I am the handmaid of the Lord." (Luke 1:38)
   Fiat . . . "Let it be to me according to your word." (Luke 1:38)
   Magnificat . . . "My soul magnifies the Lord." (Luke 1:46)
   With love and fervor, impress these words on your heart, ponder them, and act upon them.

921. When it becomes distressed, a child's first impulse will

be to call for its mother: "Mommy! Mommy!" The very word *mommy* means everything to the child. In the same way, you should learn to cry out to your mother Mary: "Mother! Mother! I love you, I trust you. You are everything to me."

922. The Rosary is a chain that binds you to your mother. It is your family album that records her journey along the Road of Hope. It recalls her love at Bethlehem and her anxiety on the way to Egypt. You see her silent labor in the home at Nazareth and her fervent prayer at the Temple in Jerusalem. You reflect on her feelings as her son preached to the crowds and as he hung on the cross with her at his feet. You can see her joy at his resurrection and her maternal love for the apostle John up to the time of her death. We can be certain that the Lord lives in his mother and she in him; their two lives are intertwined as one. Therefore, do not abandon this Rosary which she has given you. Rather, through it, learn to live like her, with her, through her, and in her.

923. There is no gift which is as precious as the gift which comes to us from the heart of Mary. She gave us our Lord Jesus Christ, the most precious of all gifts. Precious, too, is her heart, because "blessed is the fruit of your womb!" (Luke 1:42).

924. Jesus has clearly outlined for us the standard which he expects us to follow: "You, therefore, must be perfect, as your heavenly Father is perfect" (Matthew 5:48). But since no one has seen the Father, Jesus told us where we are to find him, in Jesus himself: "He who has seen me has seen the Father" (John 14:9).

And then, in order to help us to live like him, the Lord gave us the gentle and loving example of his mother Mary: "Behold, your mother" (John 19:27).

925. Even when it is faced with dangers and difficulties, a little child will continue to imitate its mother in everything. A child will watch its mother take the medicine, and take some itself. It might even follow its mother into prison. All this is not because it consciously sets out to follow her example or because it has necessarily decided that she is right about everything, but simply because she is its mother and it instinctively loves and trusts her. Our mother Mary is a shining example: The Holy Trinity has not created anyone holier than she. Therefore, learn to imitate her instinctively.

926. Mary gives us a wonderful example of a life of modest seclusion while still remaining constantly accessible to others. Throughout her life, she stayed in the background, while nevertheless always living for Jesus. Do you live entirely for the Lord as he lives for you?

927. Our Lord continues to live and act in the Church and in you. Likewise, Mary is present in the Church and to you, because she is the mother of the Church and your mother.

928. Mary was not present at the moments of glory in her son's life, such as the Transfiguration on Mount Tabor and the triumphal entry into Jerusalem on Palm Sunday. However, during the moments of greatest stress and anxiety in his life or those of his

followers—the flight into Egypt, the way of the cross, the crucifixion, the apostles' wait in the Upper Room—she was present
with all her courage and trust in God. She did not live for herself
or her own glory, but for the Lord and his work of redemption.

929. After the Ascension, Mary joined with the apostles in
prayer, preparing herself and assisting them to prepare themselves for the coming of the Holy Spirit. She prepared the way
for the public inauguration of the Church, the Mystical Body, in
much the same way as she had prepared for the birth of Jesus
Christ, its head. Truly she is Mother of the Church.

930. Throughout history, Mary could have chosen cities—with
their towering edifices and imposing cathedrals, their intellectuals
and theologians—to be the sites for her appearances. However,
she chose instead to appear to simple people in desolate locations,
choosing to come to those whom nobody else would seek in places
no one would otherwise think of visiting. In a similar way, with
utter innocence and simplicity, she wants you to come to her.

931. During her earthly life, Mary lacked almost everything that
the world regards as necessary for a happy life. When you meditate carefully on the Magnificat, you will realize that she was
truly the lowliest of the low, the humblest of servants. However,
the Lord looked upon that poverty with favor and in his mercy
made her "full of grace."

932. Mary was poor, having neither money nor possessions, and
at times she was even homeless. She was probably not what we

would consider well-educated or eloquent. However, she still had the most precious Word to present to the shepherds in Bethlehem, to the Wise Men from the East, to Simeon and Anna in the temple, and to all humanity on Golgotha. She silently gave all of them Jesus, the only gift she had to give, and this gift spoke on her behalf, because it was the gift of the Word of God.

933. Mary's total self-giving was rendered fruitful because of her complete trust in God. Contrary to the social norms of her time, she vowed to remain a virgin forever. The Most High, however, bestowed on her not only the grace of being the Virgin Mother of God, but that also of being mother of humankind.

934. You have a large heart, but a small pocket. Nevertheless, there is one gift which you can always give which will satisfy your desire to be generous. Follow the example of Mary in giving the one gift that cannot be bought, the incomparable gift of Jesus Christ.

935. When disaster strikes you, come to our mother, the Help of Christians. When you fall into sin, call on her intercession as Refuge of Sinners. Afterwards, you yourself should become like her and welcome all to take refuge with you, becoming their "life, sweetness, and joy."

936. Mary lived completely for Jesus: Her only vocation was to share in his work of redemption. All the honor she receives derives from him. In fact, were it not for the fact that she gave the world its Savior and then lived her entire life for him, her being

would be meaningless and insignificant. Likewise, your own life will be meaningless and insignificant if you are separated from Jesus.

937. Develop an appreciation for your spiritual life, a life which can find its meaning in our mother Mary. Though her life was active, her every thought and deed, no matter how small, was done for Jesus. It was impossible for her to live a single moment separated from him. So her life became one in which action was never separated from contemplation. Contemplative in the midst of activity, her actions flowed from her contemplation.

938. When Jesus triumphed in the greatest of conflicts between good and evil, Mary was there to witness the greatest revolution in history. Yet he did not come to overturn the law, but to perfect it, and Mary was there at his side at the historic moment when, by his sacrificial death, the Old Covenant gave way to the New.

939. If you love adventure, imitate the life of the Virgin Mary. Her life was nothing short of an epic journey of faith, during which she entrusted everything to God's providence. She followed where he led, whether it was to a manger in Bethlehem, a road to Egypt, a common house in Nazareth, or a desolate hill outside Jerusalem. No matter where she was, she continued to persevere in this faith, risking everything in the sure confidence of God's fidelity to his promise.

940. A life spent imitating that of the Virgin does not require you to do everything she did (no one in history can take her place) or to reenact her every movement from Bethlehem to Jerusalem. Your imitating her is not contingent on any specific place. But it does depend on your allowing Jesus to live in you and through you, in a perfect bond of love. Your life should be one continuous Christmas where you present Jesus to everyone you meet.

941. If you are a young person striving to live faithfully, follow Mary's example. In her, there remained nothing of self. Our immaculate Mother was filled with the Holy Spirit, so that we can never speak of her without thinking at the same time of the Lord.

942. Deprived of God, you would be completely empty, lonely, and miserable. Attaining a satisfactory level of human happiness hinges on maintaining communication with God. Mary's life was one of complete communion with him; she was the perfect creation according to his will. Thus, all of his gifts are most clearly manifested in her.

943. Mary's life was one of freely and happily lived poverty. She readily loved this poverty because her heart was rich and she already possessed the greatest treasure. Because of this, while she may have been materially the poorest mother, she was also the most beautiful, radiating a beauty bestowed by and derived from the Lord Jesus Christ.

944. Mary's sufferings no doubt were intensified when she was helpless. As she watched her beloved son's agony on the cross, she was completely powerless: The greater her love, the greater her brokenheartedness. Nevertheless she stood firm so that now she can protect you whenever you feel powerless in your sufferings.

945. At the foot of the cross, we see Mary attaining heroic dimensions. She was meek in her loneliness for she had lost her only son. She loved God to the point of offering her own life in union with the blood of her son to redeem the world. She was a martyr, because while she could not die with her son, she was firmly united to his death. In the face of the world which saw in the crucifixion and death of Jesus a complete and utter failure, Mary remained firm and steadfast in her faith, hope, and love.

946. When she lost her son in the temple at Jerusalem, Mary's heart suffered as she searched for him. Nevertheless, this episode allows us to see the clear manifestation of her love for him. Likewise in our lives: At the times when the Lord seems absent, then is our love for him clearly tested.

947. Love for Mary is clearly manifested by those who love her Rosary. Only those who truly love her would be able to repeat the same stories and words over and over without ever becoming bored.

948. Mary was concerned not only for the welfare of Jesus—although this was her greatest priority—but also for that of

other people: Elizabeth, John, and the bridal couple of Cana, to name just three examples. Imitate her attitude: Be concerned for the Lord, but do not forget your neighbor.

Thirty-Six: Hope

*Always be ready to explain to others
this hope which abides in you.*

949. "Blessed be the God and Father of our Lord Jesus Christ! By his great mercy we have been born anew to a living hope through the resurrection of Jesus Christ from the dead" (1 Peter 1:3).

950. Christians are light in the darkness, salt where life has no zest, and hope in the midst of a humanity which has lost its hope.

951. Remember the advice which St. Paul always gave his Christians: Do not live like people without hope.

952. As Christians, we are "awaiting our blessed hope, the appearing of the glory of our great God and Savior Jesus Christ" (Titus 2:13).

953. Many Christians leave the work of redemption to God, failing to realize that he has entrusted this task to their collaboration.

954. To be in love with God is to be in love with the world. To hope in God is to hope in the salvation of the world.

955. You must proclaim the good news to the world. This news includes not only the negative message of the commandments, but also the positive revelation of the love for the world of the God who loved and redeemed us.

956. On the cross, Jesus was very poor. Therefore, ask our crucified Lord for only three simple things: love, suffering, and hope.

957. If your reflections on these pages have not helped to fill your life with the gospel, if you are still praying "May thy kingdom not come," you will never be the hope of the world.

958. Technologically, the human race has progressed more during the past several decades than it did in all the preceding centuries. It seems an obvious conclusion to many that we now have everything at our disposal; nothing more is lacking. We have begun to think we can do anything. But amid all this, we have lost contact with the meaning of life, the direction where we are going, and what the future holds for us. So humanity in modern times finds itself in a crisis of hope.

959. God does not retreat before human progress. Quite the contrary, the more humankind grows in power and

sophistication, the more it will need hope in order to secure further progress, and the more it will need love in order to continue living. Otherwise, what would be the purpose of life? Would life be worth living? Are nihilism and hate the only legacy of our progress?

960. Some people think that the more humankind advances, the more God will recede into the distant horizon. In their hearts, they profess that "God is dead." They soon find, however, that once their consciences are "liberated," this new "liberty" sows nothing but confusion and fear. These poor souls lack hope!

961. Every age has its share of people who proclaim themselves prophets but whose message brings no real hope to humanity. Only Jesus proclaimed himself to be the way. He alone has brought a hope with worldwide dimensions, a hope that can inspire people to "Go into the whole world and preach the gospel to the whole creation" (Mark 16:15) and to be "my witnesses in Jerusalem and in all Judea and Samaria and to the end of the earth" (Acts 1:8).

962. People hope to live and to go on living, so they turn to whoever will offer them the greatest hope. Jesus gives such hope: "I came that they may have life, and have it abundantly" (John 10:10). His mother Mary is our model in hope; indeed, she is, as we often pray in the Salve, "our hope."

963. Laypeople should learn to love their vocation to the world. It is by means of this vocation that they render eternity present

in their time. They must believe that God has entrusted the world and all that is in it to their care that they may be led to eternal salvation. They must firmly believe that salvation comes only from God, but that they also have an active cooperation in this work. They must live in hope and share it with others.

964. The person of hope is a person of prayer. The object of hope is the object of prayer. The person of hope is God's co-worker. God looks to such a person to complete his work of creation and redemption.

965. We pray to God, but he relies on us. He established the Church as the instrument of salvation. This Church bears the responsibility for the completion of God's work and so is our hope.

966. There are those Christians who sit back, fold their hands, and wait for hope to come along. They passively shirk any responsibility. They look up only when they need to cry for help: Otherwise, they look neither to the future *toward* making some progress nor to the present *toward* any of their brethren who may need help. And yet because they are Christians, there is hope within them—they just refuse to see it!

967. Do not run away from your present circumstances, hoping to find something different or less difficult. If you truly believed what you profess in the Apostles' Creed about "life everlasting," you would realize that you have hope seeking to arise within you and that you will blossom forever.

968. You must live in eternity, while continuing to live entirely in the present. You should have concern for the salvation of your neighbor, but this concern should be united with God and for his sake. Strive to progress with all your strength, but do not forget to rely on the light from above. Love the world, but love with a spiritual love. And, above all, never forget to ask the question that if your heart is not filled with hope, what value will all these things have?

969. If you truly believed in your vocations as Christians, as families, as husbands and wives—your unique vocation to whatever circumstance you find yourself in—you would cease to be so easily discouraged by the difficulties you face. You would be filled with hope, because you would know that the Savior who has called you to embark on this road will lead you to its happy end.

970. We must resolve not to separate Christian life from the cultural ambiance which surrounds it by concentrating exclusively upon the things of the spirit. Rather, we must help Christians to enrich their surroundings with their spirit of hope.

971. If you should fall in your weakness, do not give up. Rise, humbly implore God's forgiveness, and continue forward. Look at the example of the boxers at a tournament who frequently succumb to repeated blows and fall. But they always get back on their feet and continue fighting, hoping finally to win the bout.

972. Can you imagine a true Christian who is not anxious to spread hope in the world?

973. "A counsel to my friends of the younger generation: Always strive to live lives of hope. If you have hope, you will always find happiness and will then be able to share that happiness with others" (Chiara Lubich).

974. You may wonder when you will be able finally to submit your resignation as an apostle and retire from the apostolate. You forget that your apostolic work, although its scope may vary with age or ability, was accepted at baptism and confirmation. Only when he hung dying on the cross could the Lord say, "It is finished" (John 19:30). It is the same for you: Only death will terminate your work as an apostle.

975. Families are the future hope of the Church. We must mobilize all their resources in answer to the call of the Church, encouraging them to proclaim the Good News to the world, a world which needs to hear their message more and more with each passing day.

976. Always maintain a sense of hope, never allowing yourself to be discouraged by the internal difficulties or petty rivalries which may arise in the apostolate.

977. Do not lose hope just because you may think you lack the means for some undertaking. I have always remembered the

words of a cardinal who said, "Use the same means as the apostles. They had no machines or equipment: They simply preached and wrote letters. And still they conquered the world." If you cannot believe this, I am afraid that your outlook has become too scientific and less apostolic.

978. A straight line consists of an infinite number of little points joined together. Similarly, a lifetime consists of millions of minutes and seconds joined together. If every single point in the line is set correctly, the line will be straight. If every minute of a lifetime is well used, the life will be holy. The Road of Hope is paved with small acts of hope along the way. A life of hope is born of every minute of a lifetime that is lived in hope.

Thirty-Seven: A Life of Hope

A few signposts to guide you home
along the Road of Hope

979. You want to have a true revolution; you desire to change the world. With the help of the Holy Spirit, you will fulfill the noble mission in life that God has entrusted to you. The key to your success will be that you prepare to make each day a new Pentecost.

980. You must work constantly for the happiness of everyone. You must unite yourself continually to our Lord's sacrifice in order to secure peace and prosperity for people and nations. In these quiet and achievable ways, you put your faith truly into practice.

981. Hold firmly to the apostolic ideal that "Greater love has no man than this, that a man lay down his life for his friends"

(John 15:13). Always be prepared to expend your energies without ceasing and to wear yourself out without thinking to win your neighbor for God.

982. Your slogan must be "Unity of All." That is, there must be unity among Catholics, unity among all Christians, and unity among nations, so "that they may all be one; even as thou, Father, art in me, and I in thee" (John 17:21).

983. Entrust yourself to one power, the Holy Eucharist, the Body and Blood of the Lord which was given that you may live: "I came that they may have life, and have it abundantly" (John 10:10). As the Israelites were fed by manna during their journey to the Promised Land, so too you will be nourished by the Eucharist as you travel along the Road of Hope to your heavenly homeland.

984. You will need to wear only one uniform and speak only one language: that of love. As a uniform, love is the sign that will identify you as one of the Lord's disciples. It is a badge that costs little, but is difficult to find. As a language, love is more important than the ability to "speak in the tongues of men and of angels" (1 Corinthians 13:1). It is the only language that will continue to exist in heaven.

985. Attach yourself to prayer as the one guiding principle. No one is stronger than the one who prays because it is to such a person alone that the Lord gave the unique assurance

of having every request granted. Whenever you are united in prayer, Jesus himself is present with you (see Matthew 18:19–20).

I earnestly counsel you to set aside one (or better still, two) hours each day, in addition to the time you already devote to formal liturgical prayer, for personal prayer. My experience over the years has repeatedly vindicated the words of St. Teresa of Avila: "He who does not pray does not need the devil to lead him astray: He will cast himself into hell."

986. Make the gospel the one Rule you observe. It is superior to all other rules and constitutions, because it was the one Jesus himself entrusted to the apostles. Unlike many other rules, it is neither difficult, complex, nor legalistic. Rather, it is gentle, simple, and dynamic, stimulating to the soul. A saint divorced from the gospel is a false saint.

987. Take your orders from one leader, Jesus Christ, by following his Vicar, the Holy Father, and the bishops in union with him. United with them, live and die for the Church as Christ did. Never forget, however, that living for the Church entails as much sacrifice as dying for it.

988. You should have a special love for the Virgin Mary. St. John Vianney once declared that, "After Jesus, my first love is our blessed mother Mary." Listen to her and you will never go astray, work for her and you will never fail, honor her and you will win life eternal.

989. Your one wisdom should be that of the cross. United to the cross, you will find the answers to the questions vexing you. If the cross is the standard by which you make your judgments, you will always be at peace.

990. Always turn to your Father who is full of love for you, following the example of Jesus whose whole life, every last thought and deed, had but one aim: "I do as the Father has commanded me, so that the world may know that I love the Father" (John 14:31).

991. There is only one thing which you need to fear: sin. During his reign as Patriarch of Constantinople, St. John Chrysostom incurred the wrath of the Byzantine court for his courageous denunciations of the empress's conduct. Various schemes were put forward to exact vengeance from the saint.

One courtier suggested throwing him in prison, but his plan was rejected by his colleagues who realized that, "There he will have the opportunity to pray and to suffer for the Lord just as he has always wanted."

Another suggested banishment, but this idea was likewise rejected: "For him, everywhere is the Lord's country."

Still another courtier suggested simply executing the troublesome patriarch, but he too was rebuffed: "If we kill him, he will be a martyr and all we will have succeeded in doing is satisfying his aspirations. . . . None of these ideas will cause him to suffer: On the contrary, he will gladly embrace any of them."

Finally a courtier observed, "There is only one thing that John is afraid of and which he loathes above all else: sin. But it is impossible to force him to commit a sin!"

If you fear only sin, nobody will be able to overcome you.

992. Cherish one desire: "Thy kingdom come, Thy will be done, on earth as it is in heaven" (Matthew 6:10). Your one desire on this earth should be that those who do not yet know your Father will come to know him here as he is known in heaven, that they will begin to love each other on this earth with the love that comes from above so that heaven may truly be found on earth. You must strive to bring this about, beginning now to share the happiness of heaven with those whom you encounter in this world.

993. Your apostolate is still lacking one element: "Go, sell what you have and give to the poor, and you will have treasure in heaven; and come, follow me" (Mark 10:21). That is, you must resolve to commit yourself once and for all—the Lord wants apostles who are free from all other attachments.

994. The most effective tool in the apostolate is personal contact. By personal contact, you enter into the lives of others in order to understand and to love them. Sincere personal interest is far more effective than all the sermons and all the books put together. Heart-to-heart exchanges are the secret of perseverance and success in the apostolate.

995. "Mary has chosen the good portion, which shall not be taken away from her" (Luke 10:42). If you are not living the interior life, if Jesus is not the very life and center of your activities, then you do not need any more instructions from me—the consequences of such a life are too obvious.

996. On this journey, your food is the will of the Father, by which you live and grow. All your actions must proceed from the will of God. It is like the nourishment which strengthens you, without which you would die.

997. You have only one moment, and it is a most beautiful moment: the present moment. Live it completely in the love of God. And if you build up your life like a crystal from a million such sparkling moments, what a beautiful life it will be! Do you not see how easy it is? It is not so difficult!

998. You will need only one strategy: the eight Beatitudes which Jesus gave us in his Sermon on the Mount (see Matthew 5:3–12). If you plan your life according to these principles, you will be filled with a supernatural joy which you will be able to communicate to all whom you meet.

999. The only task that should concern you is the fulfillment of your duty. Your duty is neither great nor small; it is what your heavenly Father has entrusted specifically to you in his plan for history. Many people today contrive all sorts of complicated ways to live the virtues and then complain that it is difficult to live them. It is not the same for you because you know that the most simple and certain path to virtue is to fulfill your ordinary duties in life.

1000. There is only one way to become holy: through your willingness to conform to the grace of God. God will never be lacking in his grace, but is your will strong enough?

1001. When God asked St. Thomas Aquinas, "Thomas, you have written well of me, what do you desire for a reward," without any hesitation, the Angelic Doctor replied, "Only you, Lord, only you!"

When you reach the end of your journey along the Road of Hope, the only reward awaiting you will be God himself.